dream
BIG

dream
BIG

How the *Second Half* of Life
Can Be the *Better Half* of Life

Patricia King

DESTINY IMAGE® PUBLISHERS, INC.
P.O. Box 310, Shippensburg, PA 17257-0310

*"Speaking to the Purposes of God for This Generation
and for the Generations to Come."*

This book and all other Destiny Image, Revival Press, Mercy Place, Fresh Bread, Destiny Image Fiction, and Treasure House books are available at Christian bookstores and distributors worldwide.

For a U.S. bookstore nearest you, call 1-800-722-6774.

For more information on foreign distributors, call 717-532-3040.

Reach us on the Internet: www.destinyimage.com.

ISBN 10: 0-7684-2625-1
ISBN 13: 978-0-7684-2625-0

For Worldwide Distribution, Printed in the U.S.A.

1 2 3 4 5 6 7 8 9 10 11 / 11 10 09 08

DEDICATION

Dedicated to the Ancient of Days.
You are full of beauty, love, wisdom, grace, righteousness,
truth, and power.
Oh how I long to be just like You!

SPECIAL THANK YOU

Special thanks in memory of Mother Teresa
who taught me to adore wrinkles…
hers were as deep and beautiful as her love.

ENDORSEMENTS

As I began to read and paragraphs turned into chapters, I was stirred deep within by faith to grab hold of all that the Lord has for me; to actually believe for the unseen to be seen; to believe for the impossible to be possible. I encourage all to read Patricia's book! You will be stirred but also taught the practical application of putting the how-to's to your destiny. I know that all who read this book will be as blessed as I was. Patricia has done a great job of putting this book together for such a time as this. This promises to be one of those books that helps thrust many into their destiny.

KEITH MILLER
Stand Firm World Ministries
www.sfwm.org

Patricia King is one of the most influential Christian women of our time. Her powerful ministry shatters the Church's gender barrier and helps move the Body of Jesus from a boys' club to the Bride of Christ! Now Patricia is after the Iron Curtain—the generational wall that has disempowered the middle aged, relegating them to spectators in the battle for history. Brick by brick she single handedly exposes lies that have separated an entire rank of people from their destinies and equips them for the victory that lies ahead. This book is a must read for everyone entering the second half of their lives.

KRIS VALLOTTON
Author of *The Supernatural Ways of Royalty*
and *Developing a Supernatural Lifestyle*
Founder, Bethel School of Supernatural Ministry
Co-leader of Bethel Church, Redding, California

Patricia King is a trailblazer, a pioneer, and a revolutionary. I have really come to love and appreciate her for the example that she is to the entire Body of Christ and to the world. Not only is she a woman full of the presence and power of God, but she is also a woman full of integrity, character, and a burning zeal for the things of God. She stands for the truth no matter what the cost, and she is a living testimony of a person who goes from "glory to glory." I recommend this book because Patricia is a great example of one who is blazing a trail of fire for Jesus in the second half of her life, and I believe that her words will set you on fire as well! May the latter years of our lives be even greater than the former as we go from one level of glory to another! It is my honor to recommend to you, my friend, Patricia King!

RYAN WYATT, PRESIDENT/FOUNDER
Abiding Glory Ministries
www.abidingglory.com

We are living in a day of great spiritual activity and, most importantly, the apprehension of divine destiny. Many saints from all spectrums, walks of life, and generations are discovering a function in God's Kingdom that is both rewarding and fruitful. Patricia King captures this reality in her book and conveys practical means to achieve lasting fruit for a multi-generational anointing. Patricia has a revelatory perspective of our present place in church history and provides key insight into mobilizing a body of people into that purpose. Every reader will find themselves drawn to the destiny for which they were born.

PAUL KEITH DAVIS, FOUNDER
White Dove Ministries

For those of you who feel as though your "best" years are behind you, this dynamic book is a spiritual torch that will lovingly rekindle the flames of your hopes, dreams, promises, and destiny into a better, brighter, and hotter bonfire than any that ever burned in your earlier years. After all, eternity lasts for a long time (forever)—you've barely taken your first breath!

JESSICA L. MILLER
Publications Manager
The ElijahList

If you want the second half of your life to be better than the first, this book is for you. Now is not the time to slow down, drop out, or fade away—and with these simple, practical keys you won't have to. This book will inspire you, and as you apply the truth within its pages, your future will look brighter and brighter!

MARILYN HICKEY
Marilyn Hickey Ministries

Patricia King is one of the most godly and courageous women I've ever met—and her victories show it. In *Dream Big* she unveils the inner workings of her courage and reveals the keys to her personal victories. This is one of the most practical books on personal triumphs and victory ever written.

BILL JOHNSON
Author of *When Heaven Invades Earth*
Senior Pastor of Bethel Church
Redding, California

Patricia King's book is a very enjoyable, encouraging book, especially for those in the second half of life. It is a very practical tool to help make attitude adjustments, fight off discouragement, and point the way to get the most out of life as a believer. Patricia helps us to understand that a "faith lift" is more important for our happiness than a "face lift." Patricia perceives the power of peace, the fallacy of fearful fretting, and the reality of rest through reconciliation.

RANDY CLARK
www.globalawakening.com

CONTENTS

This book is not for everyone—in fact it might not even be for you. It is written for those who want to live a vibrant, healthy, positive, empowered, and extremely fruitful life after 40. It is for those who are pursuing wholeness in spirit, soul, and body. It is for those who desire to be spiritually empowered, enlightened, and illumined by the Spirit of Truth. If that is you, then feel free to turn the page and begin a journey of encouragement with me...even if you aren't over 40 yet.

THE BEST IS YET TO COME!

"The latter glory of this house will be greater than the former," says the Lord of hosts, "and in this place I will give peace..."

HAGGAI 2:9

The Second Half of Life—
The Better Half of Life

The year before my 40th birthday, I was wrestling with some age issues that I had never encountered previously as I had never been age-sensitive. At the time, I was leading a mission's outreach center in Tijuana, Mexico, with most of our staff being young people in their early to mid-20s. When we hung out together in casual relational settings, they often shared with anticipation their future plans for marriage, family, educational pursuits, careers, maturing in ministry, and buying homes, along with other dreams and ambitions.

I was excited to hear their plans, but it struck me that I was soon turning 40 years of age, and I had already fulfilled all my life's goals and dreams. Everything they were longing for, I already had. I was married to a wonderful man, had two healthy teenage boys, had retired from a nursing career after working successfully in the field for ten years, was gloriously touched by God at age 25, and was fulfilled with ten years of fruitful Christian ministry. My husband and I had a large circle of amazing friends and enjoyed all the basics for a comfortable life.

The young people had so much to look forward to, but what about me? Where should I go from here? Was there anything left to experience? I wrestled that year with many internal questions. I dreaded waking up the morning of my 40th birthday. A present that had come in the mail was left on the kitchen table. Opening the gift, I discovered that it was a book for those in "the second half of life." Yikes! Did I really need to be reminded? Out of casual curiosity, I opened the introductory chapter to read: Most folks who turn 40 have at least half their life yet to live.

That statement hit me like a hammer. What a revelation! Half my life yet to be lived! If the first half was so good, then the next half must be even better. By 40 you have learned a measure of wisdom and you have gained understanding through the many tests that life offers. As a result, the years after 40 have the potential to be the best ever!

If the first half of your life was difficult, then the next half truly has great promise. All the hard lessons learned will be a springboard for success and fulfillment. If the first half was fulfilling, then the next half must be all the more so. It is a new beginning—and it can start right now. From the moment I read that first sentence of the book on my 40th birthday, a heart change took place. I determined that the second half of my life would be the best. It would be the most fruitful... the most exciting. After all, I still had time to do many things that I had never put my hand to yet.

Since then, I have pioneered many new projects and entered into a vibrant season in television and Web media production. I have authored books and study courses and produced CDs, along with traveling all over the world as an itinerant conference speaker. Our family increased as our sons married, and my husband and I became happy grandparents. I have had opportunity to pour into the next generation and help them get established. Every area of my life has increased in blessing in the second half, and as a result, I passionately desire to pass on some treasures and insights discovered along the way.

A Big Lie

Our culture preaches a lie when it suggests that aging is a negative element that must be resisted. The message is everywhere. Advertisements proclaim that wrinkles must get regular Botox injections, saggy face muscles need a surgical lift, aging men need a mega dose of Viagra, and after 50 you better look at planning to take early retirement…maybe sit back at a pool deck, sip on lemonade, and drive around in a motor home. In no way am I suggesting there is anything wrong with looking your best and enjoying recreation, but if we bow out in our prime, all the wisdom that fills our generation will be buried. I am not suggesting that we shouldn't look our best…but why do we get oppressed over a few wrinkles when maturity offers so many benefits? Why cash in the glory of our inner wisdom for a temporary outer fix-up? Let's rise up into fullness and be the most outstanding and fruitful second-half generation that has ever lived.

Most presidents, kings, queens, ambassadors, and other national and global leaders usually come into office in their second half of life. Most people become financially stable in their second half of life. By the second half of life, we have learned most of the hard lessons and have a bit of wisdom under our belts. Our gifts and talents have matured to a point where they can be utilized to their fullest potential. We are just getting started. This is no time to wind down—we are just winding up! We can anticipate blessings galore in the second half of life. The best is yet to come!

One of my favorite Bible characters is Abraham. He started following God in his 70s and began fulfilling his outstanding prophetic destiny at 100. Joshua led the Israelites into their promised land in his 70s. Daniel was in his 70s when he experienced his most significant visions. How exciting to think that your life has hardly even begun at 40.

No matter what has transpired in your journey up to this point, it can get better. This day can truly be the first day of the rest of an absolutely amazing life. No matter what age you are, no matter what path you have walked—everything can go crazy awesome for you starting right now! I have faith for you. The possibilities are unsearchable.

I was born June 26, 1951, so you can do the math. I find that every decade of life gets better—especially after 40. Expect the rest of your life to be the best ever. For those of you who have not had a life filled with goodness yet, this year could be your breakthrough year—it can be and it should be! You are precious and God wants your life filled with good things. Jesus said, "…My purpose is to give them a rich and satisfying life" (John 10:10 NLT). Life is to be really *good*…in fact, it should just keep getting *"gooder"* and *"gooder"*!

This book is full of encouragement and faith. You will see how easy it is to live a fruitful and enjoyable life. My prayer is that joy and strength will be imparted to you as you read through the following pages. This book is an easy read—but one that could change you forever—for the second half of life is truly to be the better half. The best is yet to come!

CHAPTER ONE

Attitude Is Everything

You were created to enjoy the best of everything. Think of every positive element that would make your life full and wonderful—things like: good friends, a healthy and fit body, abundance of provision, a vibrant and glowing appearance, favor everywhere you go, inner peace, dynamic spirituality, and a home and family filled with joy. Did you know that all these things are available to you? The second half of life offers you the potential to embrace all of the above and much more. In fact, it is actually much easier in some ways to secure these benefits as you mature.

There is a vital key, however, to opening the door to this bright future of potential abundance and bliss. Your latter days can be truly greater than the former if your attitude toward life facilitates it. Your perspective on life can open the door to fullness and joy or to lack and oppression. Your attitude is everything.

Are you generally a positive person or do negative and fearful mind-sets prevail in your outlook on life? Changing your attitude can set your entire life on a different course. For example, your attitude can determine whether a trial is a stumbling block or a stepping stone—it is all in your perspective and mind-set. Negative attitudes facilitate negative outcomes while positive attitudes attract positive blessings like a magnet. You can actually aid in determining positive change for your future by simply changing your attitude.

A Contrast

While working at a medical laboratory, I became acquainted with two elderly gentlemen who came for weekly blood tests. Their appointments were within 15 minutes of each other every Friday morning. One came in consistently miserable in both attitude and appearance. He was unkempt, had deep worry lines on his face, and his eyes exposed his angry heart. He was always upset about something, never had a kind word to say, and was very negative and complaining. We attempted to change his demeanor by sharing some positive greetings, but he would not engage. He was one miserable old man who looked obviously angry, oppressed, and bitter.

The other gentleman was the exact opposite. Every Friday, he came into the lab bubbling over with joy. Although suffering from diabetes and a heart ailment, he was like a ray of sunshine. His eyes sparkled with life and his face was full of brilliant joy. He walked with a cane yet there was still a skip in his step. I will never forget his weekly routine. He entered the lab greeting everyone in the waiting room, checked in at the desk, and then sat down and declared emphatically, "I am 90 years of age, and I thank God that today He has given me a brand new lease on life." Everyone smiled. He was adorable and he truly brightened the room and everyone in it.

Over a number of weeks I became well-acquainted with both these gentlemen and discovered that they had many similarities. They were both close in age. They had both experienced some tragedies in their lives and had both suffered loss. Their attitudes, however, were very different. The one could only see the negative in everything while the other searched only for the positive. The fruit of their life's attitudes was very evident. The one was miserable, bitter, and rejected. His presence in the room brought agitation, so people deliberately avoided him. The other lived in fullness of favor and joy. Everyone enjoyed him—he was like a breath of fresh air to all.

As I observed the outcome of these attitudes, my decision was made. It was a "no-brainer"—if I wanted a happy future then my attitudes meant everything. Positive perspectives are not difficult to cultivate; it is simply a matter of creating the habit of *only* thinking positive. If you are accustomed to negative thinking, then it may take a bit longer, but it is as easy as making a choice. Negativity is a very destructive habit, and the pattern of negative thinking is usually developed in childhood. The longer you tolerate negative thinking, the more ingrained these mind-sets become, and the crop of corresponding consequences increases exponentially. This pattern can be broken at any time, however, and it doesn't need to be difficult—in fact, it can be a lot of fun! It begins with a quality decision to change. If you were simply to change two or three negative thoughts a day into a positive perspective, it would make a huge difference to your life. Don't be discouraged if a new habit pattern takes time. Any change, even the slightest improvement, is better for you than none.

Negative Atmospheres Are Exhausting!

There is nothing so exhausting than to be in a negative atmosphere. As an itinerant minister, I have had the opportunity to stay in many people's homes while speaking in their region. Most homes have been absolutely delightful places to be hosted. The positive, happy environments fuel strength and refreshment and allow great relationships to be built. In the odd home, however, I could feel the tension of negativity in the air the moment I walked through the door. All it takes is one negative person in a household to release an atmosphere of oppression.

A negative attitude will always drain you of your joy, peace, and strength. It will set the atmosphere around you that ultimately affects others in your sphere of influence. Have you ever been in the company of someone who has a river of negativity, gossip, and pessimism flowing out of their mouth? I don't know about you, but it makes me want to run. One thing I have noticed is that individuals who constantly speak negatively and demonstrate negative attitudes usually don't even realize they have a problem. Everyone around them does though.

Beware of this type of environment, as it is infectious. I have seen negativity and gossip spread to entire workplaces and circles of friends. In our home and ministry, we do not tolerate negativity and gossip. If it surfaces, we always lovingly address it. If we fail to do so, it could become like a virus and spread through the camp.

In one situation I remember attempting to respond to every negative comment with the "brighter side" of things, but the other people did not get it. They just continued to confirm their negative perspective. Finally, after the third day, I gently brought their negative attitude and conversation to their attention in an attempt to help them. They looked shocked. Later on, they sent me an e-mail justifying their negativity due to the hard life they had experienced. They suggested that my confrontation had added even more pain and trauma. Negativity breeds negativity. Unfortunately, they were blinded by it.

The Power of Positive Perspective

Every time you meditate on and choose a positive perspective, you have annihilated a negative thought. You can't be positive and negative at the same time. The positive always swallows up the negative in the same way that light expels darkness. If you are proactive and determine to choose only positive thoughts, then it is impossible to have the negative prevail. When you make a decision to choose a positive outlook and perspective, do not be deceived by emotions that contradict your choice. Simply make your decision and stand on it. The feelings will come later. They will line up if you continue in your choice. In this case, your feelings don't count—your choice does.

You can easily get addicted with a holy addiction to positive attitudes due to the fact that they make you feel good inside and bear such great fruit.

The Aging Process Is Influenced by Attitude

Medical science has discovered that negative attitudes accelerate the aging process, hinder health and healing, and affect emotional and relational well-being. On the other hand, it has been determined that positive attitudes promote health, healing, and good relationships and slow down the aging process. Maybe this is what Proverbs 17:22 (NKJV) means when it says, "A merry heart does good, like medicine, but a broken spirit dries the bones."

One of the special people in life is my father. He is actually the most positive person I know. He trained himself to be this way. I will never forget when he made a new year's resolution to only think positively. I was around 11 years of age at the time he made this decision that changed his life. He was so determined to only think positive thoughts and encouraged us to do the same. Whenever we would confess something negative, he would say, "Now, don't be negative, think of something positive instead." At the time, my pre-teen mind thought he was a bit overboard. But over the years it rubbed off on me, and I am truly grateful for his positive attitudes and perspectives. He is a very happy man, now in his later years. He has walked in this quality decision for over 45 years.

My grandfather shared this fun story with me, which took place during the time that my father was developing his positive mind-sets. Dad was eating a bowl of "health food" one morning. My grandfather looked at the substance in the bowl and asked him, "Bert, what is that you are eating? We used to feed stuff like that to the pigs on the farm during the Depression." Dad went silent for a few seconds and then responded, "Well, that's probably why their coats were so shiny." Now, that is a well-trained, positive, response!

Positive Attitude Toward Your Future

Many times as people reach 40, 50, and 60 years of age, they fear for their future. How will I be able to support myself? How will I keep up with everything? What if my health fails? If you keep a positive perspective, your future will be blessed. Fear and negativity bring that which is feared and believed to pass. If you fear that you will have a troubled future, then you probably will. Negativity attracts the very essence of what it believes. As a man "thinketh in his heart, so is he" (Prov. 23:7 KJV). I have found that attitudes and perspectives create a magnetic effect. Negative attitudes draw negativity and mishap while positive attitudes draw positive results.

Think well of your future. You were not created to have a cursed life. You were created to have an abundant and blessed life. When God created mankind, "God blessed them saying, 'Be fruitful and multiply'…" (Gen. 1:22). You were made for a full and overflowing life in the earth.

Abraham didn't stop being blessed by God at age 100 or even at 175. No, the Bible says that he was "satisfied with life" right up to his dying day. He was a fulfilled man (see Gen. 25:8). This is what you are called to also. "As your days, so shall your strength be" (Deut. 33:25 NKJV).

When you think of your future, smile. It will be good. Don't listen to the lies of the world around you. You do not have many years to live within the realm of time, so make every day count. You are not here to simply watch the days go by, but you are living in the realm of time to deposit some wonderful attributes. You have special gifts to give to the world around you. Your smile. Your talents. Your wisdom. Your prayers. At 80, 90, or even 100 you can be a world changer and a history maker.

Age does not hinder your productive ability. Sometimes I dream of what I might be like in my 90s. Wow!—what a cool vision I receive. I want to be the spunkiest, wisest, cutest granny around. I want to explore new territories and step into things I have never done before. Maybe I will take up skydiving or something (just kidding...but one never knows—smile!). The younger generation will want to sit at my feet and hear of all the wonderful adventures I experienced in life...they may even glean some nuggets of wisdom. They will think I am as cute as a button and will want to dote all over me. How fun! Seriously though, what a great future awaits us if we dare to look at the possibilities.

Make investment into your future by thinking and speaking positively concerning it now. What you believe for, you can have. You are never too old to engage in new and exciting adventures and enterprises.

I met a lawyer once who graduated from law school at 70 years of age after making a career change at 60. He became the defense attorney for a famous murder trial at age 72. He won the case. It is never too late!

Positive Attitude Toward Your Appearance

Around 40 years of age, the body begins to manifest some change in skin tone and texture, hormones, metabolism, muscle tone, sleep patterns, hair loss and color, libido, and other symptoms of aging.

Although sometimes these symptoms can be discouraging, a positive attitude is everything. You will never have the body or appearance you had at 20 to 30 years of age in your second half of life. If you try to find your 20-30-year-old body you will be disillusioned. Why? Because you are not 20 or 30 any more. You are now in your second half of life—the better half. There are benefits in the second half that you did not have in your first half. Begin to explore these wonderful possibilities and set a goal to be a most outstanding "wowzer" in your generation. Don't grieve over your losses but anticipate your gains. Your body in the second half of life can be an outstanding testimony of the goodness of the Lord. Let your mature body glow and manifest glory.

I attended a friend's Bible study when I was in my 30s. One of the ladies who attended the meeting was so striking. She was full of spunk and joy, and her conversation delivered a wealth of nifty insights. In addition to her great personality and wisdom, she was absolutely gorgeous physically, although her features were not anything out of the ordinary. She was in her second half of life, but she glowed with a radiance that was indescribable. She was dressed in style with a special, unexplainable beauty about her. I was totally shocked to discover later in the evening that she was in her late 70s. I asked her what her secret was. She leaned over to me and whispered, "Love God with all your heart, keep a positive outlook…and stay away from those little-old-lady boutiques!"

Don't let the spirit of frumpiness get on you. Remember, you are a shiner in the second half of life…so go ahead and shine. Look your best—if you want, get a new look. Look in the mirror each day and speak to the person you see in there: "Wow, you are something else! You are so beautiful, so outrageously awesome—inside and out! You were gloriously created for such a time as this!" Go ahead, give it a try. Bless those wrinkles. They didn't come overnight. It took years of living on planet earth to get those lovely marks of grace. If you try to fill them in, they will come right back…so don't fight them…jump on board and love them. You are going to have them anyway (unless you want to go for the "stretched-face" look), so you may as well make the best of it. Each wrinkle can speak volumes—each one cost a great deal in life's process to get established! Maybe we should value them more.

Make the Best of It!

I have discovered that in the aging process, my skin and muscles seem to be more compliant to the force of gravity. Recently my young grandson was cuddling with me. …He stared at my throat for a while with a perplexed look and then gently and carefully grabbed some loose skin. (I was so surprised he found it, as it is such a small thing—really small—smile!) "What's that?" he questioned. "Well that's Grandma's special, secret, cuddle toy," I replied. Grandmas only get to have one of these when we get older. Isn't it nice and soft? I'll let you snuggle up to it if you're careful...but remember it is very special, so be nice."

Why moan over the sag? It's there and not all the exercise in the world can fix it completely. If you have it surgically tucked, it may be corrected for a while but will eventually find a way to sag again. So I chose to see it as a treasure...and so does my grand-son. It is all in your perspective. Why get all depressed over a small "skin sag" when you can have fun with it?

In another chapter we will cover the subject of weight control. It is common for people in the second half of life to get discour-aged with weight gain. One of the greatest keys to overcoming is to have a positive attitude. You can do it. Don't look at past fail-ures—remember that you are a winner. Love yourself and know there is nothing too hard for you. If you believe something is too hard, it will be. If you believe you can do it, you will.

Develop the inner beauty of your heart. Attributes like kind-ness, love, gentleness, purity, faith, and joy will reflect in your outward appearance. There is nothing more beautiful than a pure, kind, and loving heart. If you are positive within, it will manifest outwardly.

When you invite Jesus to come into your heart, He gives you a new life within. The Bible says that the outer man perishes but the inner man is being renewed day by day (see 2 Cor. 4:16). If you allow the inner man to get strong, that "God-life" will also reflect outwardly. In Isaiah 60:1-2 we read, "Arise, shine; for your light has come, and the glory of the Lord has risen upon you. For behold darkness will cover the earth and deep darkness the peoples; but the Lord will rise upon you and His glory will appear upon you." Wow! Now there is a great promise for all of us in the second half of life.

Imagine what you will look like when the glory rises upon you. Imagine the blessing of having His glory appear upon you! This is a true promise for God's people, so receive this by faith for your own life. God's glory is His brilliance, His splendor, His majesty! Meditate on this revelation and let your heart digest it. Believe for it. You can become a glower, a shiner, and one who radiates His awesome glory and power.

Psalm 103 gives us some keys for abundant living in the second half of life. In verse 1, David actually commands his soul to bless the Lord with all that is within him. In verse 2, he exhorts his soul to forget none of the benefits of the Lord and begins to list them. He commands his soul to think on those things that are good and positive. In verse 5, he shares that the Lord, "satisfies your years with good things, so that your youth is renewed (to renew, to make new, and to repair—from the New American Standard Bible Old Testament Hebrew Lexicon, Strong's # 2318) like the eagle." Eagles go through cycles of renewal where they go to a secluded place and tear out their feathers, pull out their talons, and beat their beaks down to nothing. They are then at the mercy of God as they wait for renewal. Brand new feathers grow, a new beak is formed, and new talons come forth. The eagle is literally made new.

Positive Words Alter Your Attitude

Each day is filled with possibility and potential no matter what age you are. Every day is unique and fresh. When walking in a positive perspective and attitude, you can expect exciting things to unfold. Whatever you look for, you will find. Your attitude and expectation will often determine the outcome of your day.

One summer on the mission field in Mexico, we stayed in a very poor community where most of the people lived in cardboard shacks without running water or any amenities. We had the privilege of staying in tents with our team of 50 and using a small, humble church building to host our meetings. There was also a small room in the church in which we cooked our "camp stove meals." I woke up around 5:00 A.M. to have my quiet time of prayer and to start the breakfast preparation. I rang the bell for the rest of the camp to arise at 7:00 and served breakfast at 8:00.

Every morning the members of the outreach team came into my little make-shift kitchen to get a cup of water to brush their teeth. A young man in his early 20s greeted me with the same confession each day. Half awake he would pour his water, look up at me, and declare, "I hate mornings. I am not a morning person!" Day after day I would listen to this emphatic decree. Finally around the fifth day, I confronted this young man saying, "You hate mornings because you choose to have that attitude. If you choose to love mornings, you could start to enjoy them." He said, "That would never happen." "Try it!" I challenged.

Each day after that, he came in for his water and went through the same routine, except he had changed his confession. He declared, "I LOVE mornings!" I detected sarcasm in his decree, but hey, it was a start. Over the next number of days he continued his confession and by the end of the summer, he was pretty perky in the mornings. Through his confession, his attitude came into divine alignment. Later, he joined our staff and even led the morning prayer meetings. A positive confession can change the way you look at your day and eventually change your attitude... even if you think you hate mornings.

We find a great key for abundant living in the book of James:

> *For we all stumble in many ways. If anyone does not stumble in what he says, he is a perfect man, able to bridle the whole body as well...And the tongue...sets on fire the course of our life...*(James 3:2,6).

The words we speak pave the way of our life—either for good or evil. The words of Jesus were always full of faith and power. In John 6:63, He said, "...the words that I have spoken to you are spirit and life." There is truly life and death in the power of the tongue. If you change your confession, it can literally change the course and outcome of your life.

In the second half of life, your days can be filled with glorious opportunities. Confess this as a reality. Look forward to each day. Expect some wonderful moments. You will find them if you look for them.

Positive Attitudes Toward Others

I love people. I was trained at a very early age to always look for the best in people, so I naturally lean that way. Every individual is unique. Each one is created with tremendous value and worth and yet each individual manifests both strengths and weaknesses, both positive attributes and negative attributes. It is easy for us to get agitated with the negative characteristics in another, but we forget that our negative attributes affect others too (although it never seems to us that our issues are as bad as another's). The way that you treat others is how you will be treated in return.

Choosing to always look for the best in another will bring great joy to your life. Even behind the toughest exterior there is a beautiful creation that God fashioned in excellence. Anyone can see a flaw in another. Because that is easy for most of us, we tend to gravitate toward that kind of focus. It takes a special person to discover and focus on the good. What a wonderful attribute in an individual to be able to discover the beautiful qualities of the inner person of another and introduce those aspects to others.

Choosing a right attitude can actually change the way you feel about people. I remember struggling with a particular young man when I was just stepping into pulpit ministry. He was a street kid whose language was very foul. He was not exercised in hygiene, and his body odor, unwashed clothes, and bad breath repelled many. He was also very challenged in his intellectual and social behavior. He liked me and always wanted to hang out, but my attitude was very negative toward him. I'm ashamed to say that I outwardly faked some levels of politeness toward him. Although polite words came out of my lips, I was actually cringing within when he showed up at a meeting. Due to severe problems with his sight, he would always get really close to me and look me straight in the eyes.

At times I would even intentionally attempt to hide from him. One evening, when I was trying to engage in one of my "disappearing acts," God nailed me and pointed out what I was doing. He spoke very clearly to my heart and said, "If you continue to reject him, he will become more rejectable to you. But if you choose to accept and love him, he will become more acceptable to you."

I was so convicted that evening that I determined to make a change in my attitude toward him. I chose to look for the wonderful hidden treasures that lay beneath the rough exterior that had been molded by his painful past. I approached him warmly that evening, inviting him to sit beside me in the meeting and to join me and my friends for coffee afterward. He was so deeply touched by this kind gesture, but what was even more significant to me was that I sensed an immediate change in the way I felt toward him. Over time, he became one of my most favorite people and a family friend. Initially he didn't change at all in outward appearance and behavior, but my attitude sure had. Over time, we noticed many changes in his hygiene and in the way he communicated. He was blossoming as an individual and everyone was noticing the difference. The beautiful grace within him had always been there, buried in the wrappings of a difficult life. All he needed was some love and affirmation to call forth the treasures within.

He became a love project for our circle of friends. He taught us many valuable lessons that confronted things in us. We had to gently teach him concerning boundaries, but once we earned his trust, he learned many things quickly.

I will never forget the day when he informed me that he was moving out of our area in order to respond to a job opportunity. I was actually sad that I wouldn't see him much any more. We all had tears on the day we prayed him off to his new adventure. My transformed perspective changed everything!

Grace Growers

Pastor and author Graham Cooke calls people who irritate the flesh our "grace growers." Perhaps you know people in your workplace, church, or neighborhood who rub you the wrong way. They can be a thorn in your side or a rose in your hand depending on how you view them. Iron does sharpen iron and some of those difficult people can expose things in you that need to be refined, changed, or seasoned. It can become a fun game if you look for ways to grow in love, patience, and wisdom in the company of your "grace growers." Take on the love challenge with a positive perspective and enjoy the outcome. Your personal "grace growers" could be your greatest gift in life if you simply give them the chance. Grace growers work to bring softness in our lives. As we age, we have opportunity to mature in our ability to appreciate others who are challenging. If we don't embrace these "gifts" then we could become hardened and intolerant. Let's get "soft"—it's a better choice.

New Friends

In the second half of life, make a point to meet new friends. It is easy to get comfortable with what has been established, but new things (including relationships) will always enhance your life with flexibility and spice. After living in the same location for over 25 years, a gentleman in his mid-50s received a job transfer and moved to a city that was about 1,000 miles away. In the former place, he had one very close friend and a few acquaintances. His wife had passed on a number of years earlier. The new employment position was difficult, as he had worked in the same plant for many years. After the move, he suffered depression mainly due to the absence of his friend. For over a year, he moped around in the discouragement of the move. Finally, he began to meet new people and get new interests. He made a decision to be flexible and change his routine. He cultivated new interests and friends. He took up golfing, tennis, and bowling. He found a church that he liked and met people in the singles group and the Bible Study. It took some effort to get out of his rut at first, as he had to make the effort to go to these events all on his own. Before long, everything began to fall into place. He suddenly found himself in the midst of many new friendships and activities that brought great joy to his life.

Don't be afraid to step into some new interests and to meet new friends. It may take some effort, but it will be worth it in the end. Keep pushing through. New relationships will keep you fresh. People are interesting; they can enhance your life. Each one is a wonderful gem to be enjoyed.

Positive Attitudes Toward Trials

Life is full of trials; everyone has them. No one is exempt. Believe it or not, trials can be your greatest tutors to a good life. Trials are always uncomfortable and never pleasant, but your attitude will make or break you in the midst of them. Your attitude will determine if you collect from the trial the "treasures of darkness and the hidden wealth of secret places" (Isa. 45:3).

I have discovered that trials run through a cycle. They have a beginning and an end. Years ago, I used to bawl and squall when I walked through a period of trial. I felt sorry for myself, constantly complained, and stressed out. I lost sleep and overate. After a number of trials, I made a great discovery: my negativity did not help the trial. My negative, complaining, and anxious attitudes did not shorten the trial or make it easier. As a result of this insight, I changed my attitude. I thought, "If this trial is going to run its course, I may as well be happy in the midst of it. There is nothing I can do about it, so I may as well enjoy life as it unfolds."

I taught myself how to look for the valuable nuggets in the darkest places in life. Trials took on a new challenge for me as I discovered that if I walked through them with right attitudes, they would actually work for me rather than against me. In the darkest of hours there were always things I could be thankful for and rejoice in. We don't have to be thankful for an adverse situation, but we can be thankful for all the good things that sustain us. For example, if a family member had an accident, you would definitely not be thankful for the accident. You could easily be thankful, however, for the strength, faith, and grace that is available to you in the midst of the trial. You can rejoice that God is with you to comfort, support, and bring you and your family through this trying time. You can be thankful that God's mercies are new every morning and that this is a powerful time to draw closer to Him.

The Bible has taught me to:

Rejoice in the Lord always; again I will say, rejoice! Finally, brethren, whatever is true, whatever is honorable, whatever is right, whatever is pure, whatever is lovely, whatever is of good repute, if there is any excellence and if anything worthy of praise, dwell on these things (Philippians 4:4,8).

If you are going through a trial, turn your mind and heart to those things that are of a positive nature. Look for the hidden nuggets of wisdom. I have found that every trial will test both your love and faith. If you choose to walk in love and keep a positive, faith-filled focus, your trials will actually graduate you to a higher level of operative grace-life following that season. If you find a person who has walked through trials well, you will find a person who has been softened and broken, yet remains strong and restfully confident. That person will have secure faith and a quiet, secure authority. They are favored and honored. These are some of the many wonderful rewards that trials can bring if we make them work for us.

As we walk through the second half of life, it is advantageous to meditate on the difficult trials of the past. Learn from any mistakes made and thank God for all you learned through them.

Plan Activities That Create Positive Effects

There are probably many activities in your life that bring you joy and pleasure. What are those things? Which activities fuel you with strength and which things drain you of emotional and physical energy? The more you can fill your days with activities that create positive environments, emotions, and mind-sets, the stronger you will be physically, relationally, and mentally.

Plan your monthly schedule with activities that you love and look forward to. This adds joy to your life, and joy gives you strength. If jogging is a positive experience for you, then jog. If cleaning your house brings you satisfaction, then go for it (you can clean mine too if you would like). Perhaps window shopping at the mall is an enjoyable experience for you, or going out for dinner and a movie. Others may enjoy a game of golf, baking, working on a craft, going to the gym, playing board games, or attending a conference.

The activities that produce stress in your life need to be examined. Some of them cannot be avoided or eliminated, but others can. If you have stressful activities in your life that cannot be eliminated, then attempt to have a really good, positive attitude about them. In addition, surround your life with other things that bring you pleasure. Don't let anything rob you of your positive outlook. Choose to see the bright side in everything!

Are You Ready To Make a Quality Decision?

Why not make a quality decision right now to focus on things that are of a positive nature? It will make such a difference to your life. Years ago, a song became popular. It went like this: "Don't worry, Be happy." That pretty much sums it up doesn't it? So, let's do it! "Don't worry, Be happy"—for the rest of your life. Remember, the second half is the better half…enjoy the discovery.

CHAPTER TWO

Vibrant Spirituality— The Foundation

During my nursing career I worked a fair amount of time in a cardio ward where cardiac arrests were common occurrences. At times, after we resuscitated individuals they would share their out-of-body, after-death experiences. It was always a very similar description. I remember one gentleman sharing how he felt his spirit leave. He was still "in the room" when the heart monitor alarm sounded and we all poured into the room. He watched from the unseen realm as we successfully engaged in cardiac massage and drug administration. He felt himself returning to his body.

Your spirit man is the part of you that gives you life. When that life leaves, you have expired. Our physical body shuts down when that life leaves. Your physical body is kept alive by the spirit. When you look at a corpse, you see only the shell of the person.

The life or "spirit" has departed. Your physical body is temporal and subject to time, but your spirit is eternal and lives forever.

As you grow older, you begin to think more about the life that awaits you after you finish your course within the realm of time. You begin to experience the loss of some of your friends and family members as they leave this life, and you are left facing many questions that you probably didn't consider much in your youth. Your spiritual well-being becomes more of a focus to you in the second half of life as you ponder the vast sphere of eternity and the mysteries that fill it.

In our Western, academic culture, we have for the most part neglected the health of our spiritual nature, and yet a healthy spirit is so vital to living a full and vibrant life. In the last number of years, there has been an obvious growing hunger in the masses to search for a Power that is greater than themselves. Folks are looking for answers to life and are seeking out supernatural encounters and help for spiritual fulfillment.

If you feed your spirit good food, then everything else in your life functions better. If you are full of vibrant life within, it will manifest in other areas of your life, such as your physical health and strength, relationships, and emotional and mental well-being. Your spiritual condition often determines your prosperity as well. It is definitely very important to nurture your spirituality.

My Journey

I experienced spiritual renewal in my mid-20s during a very dark season in my life. Everything was out of control and spiraling into destruction. During that time I sought out many spiritual teachers, counselors, books, cults, and sects in order to find inner peace. For me, the initial search brought even more devastation. Although everything I encountered was enjoyable in some ways, it lacked good fruit as the symptoms of destruction increased during this season. You can always tell if something is good or not by examining its fruit. A good tree cannot bear bad fruit.

I believe that God honors a true, searching heart—and I definitely had that! One night I encountered a life-changing experience in the midst of my brokenness. I discovered that night that Truth was a Person. Jesus Christ came into my heart as I invited Him to take control of my shattered life. I felt His love fill me so completely and knew beyond a shadow of a doubt that all things had become new within. I was so touched by this unconditional, undeserved love and mercy that I stayed up all night and wept. I was so full of joy. I had truly been given new life! I discovered that everyone who calls upon His name can have this wonderful life—it is a free gift. He is not a respecter of persons. He loves everyone.

I had searched out many religious activities before experiencing this glorious God-encounter. But having a personal relationship with Jesus is very different from religion. Religion is about our behavior and works. It is about structure and forms, while Jesus is about an intimate relationship with our Creator. Christ is both Savior and Creator. When you actually meet Him, you know that your spiritual search is over. In the Bible, Jesus is called the King of kings, the Lord of lords, and the God of all spirits. There is no one like Him. He is the only way by which man can be reconciled to His Creator. I know that some of you may think that is very dogmatic thinking, but Jesus Himself made this claim, and it is truly what I believe and what I experienced. I know, that I know, that I know. I have no doubt. Man didn't give me this revelation and man cannot take it away. When you know this, you know it!

Relationship with God is very different from attending church or a meeting with other believers, although congregating can be very uplifting and valuable to keep you supported in faith. Relationship with God, however, is just that—a relationship. He is real and tangible and you can encounter Him by faith.

I realize that some readers may not share this belief. One thing I know for sure though: if you are truly searching to experience Truth with a heart of humility, you will find it...you will find Him...and your life will never be the same.

In the Appendix of this book, I have included a short booklet called *God Loves You With an Everlasting Love.* This booklet will explain the best news you have ever heard and will introduce you to this new life. If you would like to know if Jesus truly is God then simply ask Him to reveal Himself to you—and He will!

Food for Your Spirit

The Bible is not primarily an intellectual or academic book, although it is full of accurate history and insight that will challenge the best of intellectuals. It is actually a spiritual book. Within its pages and verses are layers and layers of divine revelation and truth. Meditating on the Word will bring life and encouragement to your spirit, mind, and emotions.

The Scriptures have been around for a long time. Over time it has been proven that people and nations who live by its principles live good lives.

Before reading the Bible, ask the Holy Spirit to grant you the spirit of wisdom and revelation that you may spiritually discern the truth found in its pages. Look for the wonderful insights that He wants to share with you. At times it will be as though the words you read were written by God personally for you and only for you. It can actually be that personal and that impacting.

The more you read the Bible and meditate on its verses, the more your spirit will be strengthened and your mind will be renewed. The Bible is like food for your spirit. All the promises of the Word are for everyone who believes in Christ—glorious promises that support a good life. The promises are true whether you are one year old or 100, and they are eternally true whether you believe them or not. Believing in the promises, however, is what brings the substance of their reality into your experience. For example, the Scriptures promise me that God will supply all my needs according to His riches in glory by Christ Jesus (see Phil. 4:19). That is true whether I believe it or not, but it will become manifest in my life when I believe it by faith and receive it personally.

I like making daily declarations of the Word because it is so powerful and uplifting. The following are some attributes and benefits of the Word of God:

1. It is eternal in the heavens. Jesus said that even though the heavens and the earth would pass away,

His word would never pass away. (See Matthew 24:35.)

2. When the Word is declared it does not come back empty but actually is released in the realm of the spirit to accomplish its purposes. So as an example, let's say that you declared over the storms of your life: "Peace, be still." That word, released in faith, will go forth and accomplish the peace and stillness. It will not return void without accomplishing the purpose for which it was sent. (See Isaiah 55:11.)

3. The Word builds an invisible framework of blessing around your life. In Hebrews 11:3 the Scriptures teach us, "By faith we understand that the worlds were prepared [framed] by the Word of God, so that what is seen was not made out of things which are visible." So when I declare the Scripture that promises, "Blessings will come upon me and over-take me" (Deut. 28:2-14), that framework goes to work around me so that the blessings become my portion. The blessings materialize because they were first set into place through the declaration of the Word of God.

4. The Word is like seed. When you plant a seed it grows into a full-blown plant according the nature of the seed. If I plant through declaration of the Word over my life that "grace is multiplied over me," then that seed of the word will grow that promise in my midst. (See Mark 4:1-20.)

5. The Word is a lamp unto your feet and a light unto your path and will illumine your understanding with truth so that you will not stumble in life. (See Psalm 119:105.)

6. Angels carry out the Word of God, so when they hear it decreed, it dispatches them to go to work on your behalf. Usually you cannot see or experience angels with the natural senses but they are with you. More and more people are having angelic encounters in these days. In the Bible, it was not uncommon for people to experience the appearance of angels. So get ready! (See Psalm 103:20; Hebrews 1:14.)

7. The Word is a weapon of warfare. When you are contending for breakthrough in your life and you feel resistance, the decreed Word becomes a powerful weapon on your behalf. I have seen many a battle settled by simply speaking the truth of the Word of God into the situation. (See Ephesians 6:17; 2 Corinthians 10:3-5.)

8. The Word ensures answers to prayer. When you pray according to that which is promised in the Word, your prayers are heard and answered according to John 15:7.

9. The Word brings cleansing and refreshment to you. Meditating on the Word will renew your mind and will strengthen your spirit. (See Ephesians 5:26; Romans 12:2.)

10. The Word creates. God created everything in the heavens and the earth through His Word. He spoke everything into being. When He said, "Let there be light," there was light. His Word is still creative to this day. When you declare light into your darkness, things will shift for you and light will come. You too can call things that are not as though they are. (See Romans 4:17; Genesis 1:1-3.)

Reading the Word, studying the Word, and meditating on the Word are so uplifting. When the Holy Spirit highlights and reveals the truth in the Scriptures, it creates faith within you. "Faith comes by hearing, and hearing by the Word of Christ" (Rom. 10:17).

I make it a discipline in my life to read the Bible every day in a quiet place. I also like to carry a little Bible in my purse so I can read it whenever I desire. I travel on airplanes a great deal and love to take that quiet time during traveling to read the Word.

Read a little of the Bible every day and feed your spirit. Special revelation is waiting in its pages for you. In the Appendix of this book, I have included for you part of a copy of a little booklet I wrote called *Decree*. Declare these Scripture promises over your life each day if you wish, and you will find they will renew and refresh you. These biblical decrees are ones I have made over my own life for many years.

Invest into your latter days. The more Word you sow into your life, the more light and blessing will manifest. Your latter glory will surely be greater than the former!

Prayer

Prayer is simply communicating with God. It is when you share your heart with Him and He shares His with you. You don't have to deal with life's frustrations alone or try to figure them out in your own mind. Take some time to share your heart with God. He loves hearing from you. Jesus said that if we asked the Father in His name, we would be heard and our prayers would be answered. (See John 14:13-14.)

I love prayer. In order to help people in their prayer lives, I have made CD teachings available on the many various types of prayer. But your prayer life does not need to be complicated. It is not important to learn a technique as much as it is to be real in His presence. Your prayer life will keep you vibrant. All your worries and fears can be brought to the Lord in prayer. You can let go and let God so that your life is not burdened. Simply give your burdens to Him. Once you pray, leave it with Him to sort out. Let go and let God!

You can pray for anything that pertains to life and godliness because, in Christ, these promises have already been granted you. It is like they are waiting for you to come and get them. Be bold when you pray. Ask this year for things that will bless your future.

One day not that long ago, I looked at a friend of mine who was in her 50s and she looked so much younger than the last time I saw her. I asked her what her secret was. She answered, "Prayer." She explained to me that she had found the Scriptures that promised her refreshment, strength, and restoration of youthfulness. She had prayed these Scriptures every day and they started to manifest in her life. (See Psalm 103:5; Isaiah 40:29-31.)

Don't be afraid to ask largely of God. He is a big God and is excited to co-labor with you. He loves it when His children trust Him for big things.

Worship

You were made to worship; you innately understand that there is One who is greater than you who is worthy of your worship. Everyone, in the deep place of the heart, longs to worship. To worship means to adore, to exalt, to lift up, to honor and praise another who is deserving of respect. It involves deep adoration and affection. God is worthy of worship.

When we exalt the Lord, it brings us into His world. That is one of the reasons why He loves it when we worship Him. He wants us to be close to His heart, but He doesn't force Himself on us. He waits for us to come to Him with our own free will. Then He bestows on us the blessings of that intimacy.

The Lord revealed to me once that when I worship Him for a particular attribute, it gives Him the place to establish that attribute in my life. So when I worship Him for His purity and wisdom, it gives Him the place to bestow purity and wisdom on me and to cover me with those attributes of His character. As you give to Him, He pours back into you the very thing you sow into His heart.

A Clean Heart

A pure heart is so beautiful. The Scriptures teach us that the pure in heart will see God (see Matt. 5:8.) King David asked God to create a clean heart within him after he had made some serious mistakes (see Ps. 51:10). You were created for purity; without even knowing it sometimes, you long for it.

Throughout our lives, we compromise values. As we do, we lower the bar and allow impurities to fill us. When I look at young children who have not yet been exposed to the cruelties and vices in the world and the flesh, I see such innocence. Their eyes are so pure you can look right into their innocent soul. We were created for this innocence. It was never to be lost. When a child is finally exposed to the world's rebellion, lies, and lust, however, you can see its tainting effect on them and the defilement begins. The purity is lost.

I recently was looking into the eyes of a beautiful Christian man who had kept his heart pure in his latter years. His eyes were like crystal blue and so clear. They reflected the purity of his soul. The same day, while I was in a public place, an older man lustfully stared my body up and down as I walked by him. Feeling defiled, I stopped, turned, and looked into his eyes. He walked away quickly. There was such darkness on him. Both men were about the same age. One had watched over his heart and the other had not. You cannot hide what is in your heart forever. In the second half of life, it all starts to show.

All your past mistakes can be washed away if you ask God to forgive you. You can start a brand new life and put the past behind you. My CD course, *Catching the Thief*, teaches individuals how to submit their lives to this beautiful cleansing process. It is not difficult. God makes everything simple. Anything in your life that is a violation of the basic Ten Commandments will hurt you, but it can all be cleansed, right now. Simply ask Him to forgive you and to cleanse you from all unrighteousness. When you humble yourself before Him, confess your mistakes, and receive His forgiveness, then you are ready to move on. Watch over your heart with all diligence, for from it flows the issues of life (see Prov. 4:23).

Toxins to Avoid

Defiling toxins of the soul such as bitterness, unforgiveness, offense, and critical and judgmental attitudes can create deep misery in your life. They should be avoided at all costs if you desire to have a life filled with blessing and freedom. Unforgiveness, for example, if left unchecked, will lock you up in a prison of resentment and mental torment. Bitterness and offense along with unforgiveness can destroy and erode your physical and emotional health. Critical and judgmental thought patterns will set you up for rejection by others as well as close doors of opportunity for you. People don't trust a person who is critical of others for long as they understand that a person who judges others will eventually turn on them and betray them too.

Critical attitudes become a habit. You cannot entrust your heart to a critical, bitter, and unforgiving person who is given to offense—and you shouldn't. No one enjoys being around such an individual, although sometimes it is tolerated. Such people do not even guard their own heart, so don't think they will be sensitive to yours. Ultimately isolation takes place in their lives and of course that breeds more pain which breeds more of the above. There are few things more uncomfortable than being around a person who has filled their life with these poisons. The cycle must be broken and it can be broken.

You don't need to remain in these trappings. You choose to be in them or to come free from them. The decision is yours. There is no time like right now, this very minute, to make a quality decision to change. If you found out today that you were eating poisoned food that would strip you of your health and kill you, you would be wise to stop eating the poisoned food and eat something that would promote good health. It is the same with spiritual food. If you eat spiritual poison it will surely destroy you.

I have heard some say, "That person offended me." It is actually impossible for someone to offend you, as offenses are not given, they are taken. If you are offended it is because YOU took it. It is your choice to be offended.

Unforgiveness is the same. The Bible teaches us to forgive in the same way as the Father has forgiven us. You have hurt many people in your life even if you didn't mean to. We all have, often without knowing it. You have made mistakes that have made life uncomfortable for both yourself and others. *If* you are reading this right now thinking, "Not me. I have never hurt anyone. I have only done well for people all the days of my life," then you are probably disillusioned. There is only One who is perfect and it is not you. We have all made mistakes; we all need to be forgiven.

The good news is that we have been forgiven of all our mistakes, shortcomings, and sins. Jesus asked the Father on our behalf 2,000 years ago, and He did it. All our sins are forgiven. There are two things, however, that hinder us from receiving this benefit of complete and forever forgiveness.

First, if we don't receive His forgiveness for ourselves then although it was given to us 2,000 years ago, it won't do us any good. It is like giving a loved one a new luxury car full of bells and whistles as a gift. If they never acknowledge or receive it, then how can it benefit them? It could sit on the street in front of their home for years and collect dust. It is legally theirs, but they have never received it, and therefore will never enjoy its benefits.

Second, the Bible teaches us that if you do not forgive others their mistakes, then you will not be forgiven either (see Matt. 18:23-35; Matt. 6:12). I can't afford that for a minute. I need a lot of mercy because I have made many mistakes in my life. If I want to be forgiven of all my sins, mistakes, and failures, then I must forgive others of theirs. This is not an option. The moment I hold another in a heart of unforgiveness, I have put my own soul in jeopardy. Some have struggled with forgiving as they believe it would not be just to allow the offender to go free. When you forgive someone, you are not letting them off the hook, but you are getting their hook out of you. God takes care of the rest. He is the judge of all. If we choose to judge the person ourselves, then we also will be judged by the same measure.

I have learned to not be shocked when people hurt me. It is simply human nature. We all have the potential within us to hurt others—and we all have. It is the ugliness of human flesh. It is rotten to the core. My position is not to judge them in return but to forgive, to love, and to allow the situation to make me a better person.

Being in the public eye, has given me many opportunities to test my "love levels." A person's maturity in life is measured by how much they love. An individual's true beauty is measured by their love meter. The "beauty contests" of the second half of life have little to do with outer appearances—they are mainly about love and purity of heart which in turn are reflected in the outer man. This is what we can look forward to. You may be known for many things, but if you run your course in life and are known for your love then there is nothing greater. This is the ultimate beauty contest. There is nothing more beautiful than love.

In the power of love, you will find no unforgiveness, no bitterness, no resentment, no critical attitudes, and no offense or judgments. You will instead find patience, mercy, kindness, forgiveness, support, joy, peace, and gentleness.

You can be such a person in the second half of life. Let all resentments and bitterness from the past go. Holding on to these things has not helped or protected you up to this time. Forgive those who have hurt you so that you can also be forgiven. Your Father in Heaven will sort out the situations you are dealing with. He is the ultimate Judge who is righteous and just in all things. Don't take things into your own hands but let Him sort it all out. Your inner peace in this stage of life is very important.

Let love be your greatest aim.

The Secret Place

The most important posture in life is our personal quiet time with the Lord. When reading the biographies of well-known revivalists, we find that their secret for the manifestation of the power they walked in was found in their personal prayer and devotional times with the Lord. Whatever you focus on will empower you.

When you focus on the Lord, then His Presence, wisdom, and love will empower you.

When Jesus visited the home of Mary and Martha, Mary sat at His feet to listen to Him share while Martha was distracted by her preparations. Jesus kindly explained to Martha that Mary had chosen the better posture that would not be taken from her (see Luke 10:38-42).

Life is full of distractions and things that grab our attention and focus. The quiet time that we spend each day with Jesus, learning of Him, worshipping Him, and soaking in His love is the best choice for us as it was for Mary. Time in His Presence will bring great fruit. Jesus is the vine and we are the branches. As we abide in Him, we will bear much fruit (see John 15:1-7). As every year progresses, your life can be filled with more and more fruit. The place of quietness and intimacy with the Lord is where this is all birthed.

If you are not yet used to spending time with the Lord, you may want to start by setting apart 15 minutes each day to pray, read some Bible verses, and worship. Your desire to meet with God will grow and grow the more you set this time apart. When distractions come, overcome them by making a list that you can tend to later. Tell yourself, "This is my time with God...I will look after the business of the day later, but this is my most important time."

Keep Your Faith Fresh

All things are possible if you only believe. There is nothing too difficult for God. As we grow older we must take a stand against cynicism and skepticism. Too often the aged get set in their ways and mind-sets and fail to expand in their thinking and beliefs. We find this in many churches. When God reveals new things concerning Himself and His ways, often we find resistance even in His Church. People will say, "No, He can't do that. That is not the way we learned it." This has happened over and over all throughout Church history.

God is big and great. The possibilities of what He can do and will do in and through our lives are endless. As you enjoy the second half of life, keep your faith fresh and alive. Believe for the impossible to manifest. Allow your understanding of life and God to grow and expand. The Scriptures say that His ways are past finding out. Develop an approach to life that loves to explore new territory and dares to believe. Don't get all stuck in narrow-minded ways.

Associate with people of faith and vision. They will fuel you with fresh passion and zeal. There is so much to discover in God that it will take much more than a lifetime to see it all unfold. Believe.

Fellowship

One burning coal on its own won't burn bright for long, but when it is with others it can become part of a blazing fire. Relationship with other believers is important to our faith. I find that when I connect in conversation with others who are spiritually hungry that it actually escalates and challenges me into higher places in God. I love fellowship. I love being around those who have experienced the Lord in powerful ways.

There are many good houses of worship where you can meet other believers, receive encouragement, and develop meaningful relationships. Much of my life is spent in Christian conferences. I love them! It is a time when I get to meet so many passionate believers. The hungriest of the hungry seem to flock into conferences, so the spiritual atmosphere in such environments is over-the-top. I am always so built up, and I love meeting many wonderful people at each one. In the second half of life, good wholesome fellowship with others is a great gift and source of strength and encouragement.

Exploring the Realms of the Supernatural

The Bible is full of accounts of the supernatural working of the Holy Spirit. Jesus modeled a life in the supernatural that evidenced healings, miracles, deliverances, signs, and wonders. Today, we see believers doing the same works that Jesus did. Let's examine the following Scriptures that confirm to us that believers are to do the same works today as He did then:

"...as the Father has sent Me, I also send you." (John 20:21).

"...he who believes in Me, the works that I do, he will do also; and greater works than these he will do; because I go to the Father." (John 14:12).

"These signs will accompany those who have believed: in My name they will cast out demons, they will speak

with new tongues…they will lay hands on the sick,
and they will recover." (Mark 16:17-18b).

In these days, we will see the manifestation of the power of God escalate in the earth. Just like Jesus, the company of those who perform His miraculous works will increase. Visions will increase. Angelic visitations will increase.

God often called those in the second half of life to manifest His power, engage in divine visitation, and greatly influence their generation. Moses was well over 50 when he met God at the burning bush and manifested signs and wonders before Pharaoh. Noah was not a young man when he completed the ark. Zacharias was advanced in years when he received an angelic visitation revealing that his wife Elizabeth, who was also advanced in years, would give birth to John the Baptist. Paul walked in the weight of his heavenly appointed apostleship in his second half of life.

Today, those in the second half of life who are open to the fresh move of the Spirit are being powerfully used to move in the supernatural dimensions of the Kingdom of God. The Spirit of God is being poured out afresh and glorious things are taking place. Many are encountering angelic visitations. Open visions, trances, and the heavenly realm are being experienced. Miracles of healing, deliverance from demonic strongholds, and the raising of the dead are also signs being evidenced. What a glorious hour! It is just like in the Bible—and all are invited to partake.

Don't allow your spirituality to become stale. Seek the Lord for the fresh wind of His Spirit. Open your heart to fresh revelation— God's ways are beyond anything that we can discover in a lifetime.

He will empower you with a fresh touch of His presence if you desire. No matter how old you are, He has need of you and wants to reveal more of Himself to you. Remember that His ways are beyond finding out. There are always fresh things regarding Himself and His Kingdom that He longs to reveal to those who are hungry.

In our conferences we have been so blessed by the Lord. We have seen spectacular signs, wonders, and miracles. The Bible is full of these amazing demonstrations of His glory, so why shouldn't we see them in our lives and in the Church in these days?

I love spiritual experiences. The realm of the supernatural is exciting—we were created for it!

Personal Mission Encounters

Everyone is commissioned to take God's love and truth to the world around them. Even as a pond goes stagnant if it has nowhere to flow to, so also our lives stagnate when we do not reach out to serve and bless others.

Each day you can look for ways to bless others. This will enrich your life tremendously. Invite the Lord to show you how you can serve others. Sometimes it is so simple.

When my children were young I was confined to the home most afternoons while they napped. I asked the Lord to give me ideas on how to bless others. Sometimes He would put it on my heart to write a note of encouragement or to call someone who I knew was lonely. One time I took a bouquet of flowers to a neighbor. Other times I shared baked goods or invited people over for a meal. They were simple things, yet meaningful to the recipients.

It feels so good to bless others and enriches our own lives tremendously.

The second half of life offers you many of these types of opportunities. I knew someone who began volunteering in a nursing home after they retired from secular employment. Another volunteered with the Red Cross blood donor clinics. Others in their second half of life have traveled to developing nations to help with the many needs in orphanages or mission centers amongst the poor. Still others join local outreach teams through their churches. It is very rewarding to make your life a blessing to others.

In our Western culture, we have so much. It is a privilege to give to others who are not as blessed. May our eyes be open to the needs so that we can make a difference in the lives of others.

CHAPTER THREE

Dream Big—
The Importance of Dreaming

When I speak in this chapter about dreaming, I am not talking about the dreams we have when we sleep at night. I am talking about the dreams that lie in the depths of our heart—our aspirations and desires. The second half of life is the most important time to dream big, and yet often it is when we dream less. Sometimes people think, "Why should I even try dreaming? After all, I am getting older. The time has gone." This is a total lie! It is never too late to dream. In fact, the Scriptures say, "...Your young men shall see visions, and your old men shall dream dreams" (Acts 2:17). It is never too late to stir up fresh dreams. Increased blessing in life always begins with dreaming. Dreaming will keep your life fresh and flourishing.

I mentioned earlier that when I turned 40, I was discouraged because I had fulfilled my life's goals and desires already. My husband and I took time in that season to set new goals and vision. There is always more available for you to experience.

Some in their second half of life are discouraged because they have not yet fulfilled any dreams. Sometimes this is because they have not dared to dream or walk through the process of fulfilling those dreams. It is important to have clearly defined dreams and visions within you and a plan of action to fulfill them. Remember, all things are possible!

What Is a Dream?

A *dream* can be defined as: *that which is longed for, a vision or desire, an aspiration.*

Take time to connect with the dreams, visions, and desires of your heart. Don't be afraid to let those dreams come alive within you no matter how big they might seem to you. God created you with the ability to dream and imagine. He will help you to align your vision with His will if you trust Him for this through simple faith. It is a wonderful thought to know that the Master of creative vision is present to help you.

Take time to write down some desires, thoughts, and aspirations for various areas of your life. Remember to dream big. Don't limit yourself due to things that look like obstacles—write out your dreams as though there were no obstacles at all. After you have finished, read over your dreams again and ask yourself,

"Is this possible?" In most cases, you will find yourself thinking, "Well, yes...I think it just might be possible."

Dare to believe and discover fresh excitement rising up within you at the very possibility of your dreams being realized. You were created to dream. You need to dream.

Dealing With Unfulfilled and Broken Dreams

Sometimes, people in their second half of life are afraid to step out and dream due to failures in the past. Do not let the past hinder you. Remember you are wiser now. You have gained insight. Don't be afraid or held back by previous negative experiences where your dreams and desires were aborted. You have gained insight; this is a new day. Take courage!

Take a few moments to think back on dreams that were crushed or lacked fulfillment. Write them down so that that they are well-defined. Beside each one write down how the failure to fulfill the dream made you feel. Were you angry? Hurt? Disappointed? Afraid? Self-condemned? Humiliated? Did you make any vows to yourself like, "I will never dream again!"?

Although these responses are very understandable, they can become hindrances to living in the blessings ordained for you if you do not deal with them properly. Everyone suffers disappointments, some very serious and grievous, *but we must move on or we will live our entire life with a bitter and frightened soul that produces more disappointments and pain.*

King David shared his heart in Psalm 131:1 (NIV), "I do not concern myself with great matters or things too wonderful for me." He committed things to God that were too difficult for him to understand. Sometimes we will never know the answer to the hard situations we have experienced in life, but we were never created to live with the anxiety, offense, and bitterness that comes as a result of holding it all in.

In the midst of absolute agony, Job was able to trust God even though he did not understand. In the midst of his despair, he proclaimed a sacrifice of praise: "Blessed be the name of the Lord." (See Job 1:21.) After the grueling trial, Job went on to have a good life. He had suffered much and lost much but he did not look back. The rest of his life was enriched with bounty and fullness. His end was better than his beginning, and yours can be too.

Sometimes it is healing to write a letter to God sharing your heart and your pain. Express your real feelings on paper. This gets it out of the hidden places of your emotional memory banks. If you choose to write such a letter, do not hold back. You will never mail it. God has big shoulders and a great heart. He loves you and wants you free. Expressing the pain and anger that has dwelt in your heart is often like releasing poison out of your system. It helps you to see clearly what has actually been hidden inside your heart. Once you know what you are dealing with, healing can begin. You have a clear target.

After you have expressed your honest feelings on paper, then go back over them and identify each issue. Start by forgiving yourself and anyone else who may have hindered your dreams from bring realized. Remember that unforgiveness is like poison in your soul and will keep you confined in an emotional prison. It is important to forgive. It is equally important to repent from any judgments you have made toward anyone who has hurt you. When you judge another, you are setting yourself up to be judged in greater measure. It is a spiritual law. Whatever we give to others, it will be dealt to us in return—pressed down, shaken together, and running over. As you go through this exercise, you may identify some roots of anger. Anger usually surfaces as a result of injustice. Identify the injustice and direct your anger toward the actual injustice but remove it off of any individual who was involved.

Sometimes we even judge God for our failures. Even though we don't understand at times why dreams, desires, and prayers are unanswered, God can never be judged. He loves you very much and understands your disappointment, but it honestly was not His fault. One day you will fully understand. You will never need to forgive God because He has never done wrong, but you will need to repent from any judgments you have made against Him. We never want to be God's judge. That is a serious mistake but it can be rectified by repenting and receiving His forgiveness.

To *repent* means "to turn away from." If we repent from unforgiveness and judgment then we turn away from those mind-sets. You can take care of this by first, making a quality decision to change your thoughts, and second, committing these things to prayer and allowing the Lord to take them from you. Once these things are committed to the Lord, then even if thoughts and feelings of unforgiveness and judgment return, you simply renew your commitment and remind your mind and emotions that you have made your decision.

A simple prayer like the following can aid in your process of repentance:

Dear Heavenly Father,

I confess that I have held unforgiveness and judgments in my heart toward myself, others (make mention of the people you have judged), and You. I choose to repent and turn from these judgments and all unforgiveness I have harbored in my heart. I choose to forgive everyone who has hurt me, and I choose to forgive myself. Thank You, Father, for forgiving and cleansing me from my mistakes. In the name of Jesus I pray. Amen.

Inventory of the Situation

A number of years ago, a friend of mine was involved in an investment scam. In good faith he had invested his life's savings, mortgaged his home, and cashed in insurance policies in order to enter an investment that promised outrageous returns. Since he trusted the individual who invited him to invest, it all sounded exciting. He knew others who had invested and, as a result of doing well, had rolled over the returns and reinvested. On paper, it looked like every investor was making enormous returns. At the end of a two-year season, however, everyone (including my friend) who had money in the system, lost everything invested. The situation was a scam that resulted in many legal suits and many losses. My friend had worked hard to gain what he had in life prior to this investment and now it was all lost. His home was lost, his reputation was tainted, and all his assets were gone overnight. Depression hit him hard.

Now, this is a very difficult situation and anyone could be bitter over it. I can't imagine the agony of such a situation. What does one do at a time like this?

You learn the lessons you need to learn through the tragedy and start all over! Life is full of pleasure and goodness; each day will greet you with new opportunities. Your attitude and perspective is very important at a time like this—remember, all things can work together for good. If you hide yourself inside the remorse and pain, you will stay in that pit, or you can rise up and enjoy the rest of your life.

Shake the dust off and move forward. Look over the situation and glean the treasures of wisdom learned from the mistakes. You will be a richer person for it in the end. Don't waste your sorrows; make the place of devastation into a fertile field. Make an inventory of the situation. Revisit it, and see where mistakes were made. Don't leave any stone unturned. The nuggets of wisdom and discernment that can be gleaned from times like this are priceless—they hold much more value than natural substance. As you go through this personal inventory, humble yourself and repent from any mistakes you made. Ask the Lord to forgive you and wash you clean from the negative effects of it. If you have made mistakes that hurt people, don't cover these up but go and humble yourself. Make things right to the best of your ability. Then you are ready to move forward. It is never too late to start over. It takes courage, but courage is available to you in Christ. Ask the Lord to fill you with fresh vision and enthusiasm. He will!

Pursue, Overtake, and Recover All

King David arrived in Ziklag to find that it had been severely attacked by the Amalekites and absolutely everything was lost. All the men, women, children, animals, gold, and silver—everything—was gone and the city had been burned. In David's distress he sought the Lord on what he should do in the midst of such loss. The Lord answered, "*Pursue*, for you shall surely *overtake* them and without fail *recover* all" (1 Sam. 30:8b NKJV, emphasis mine).

David went on to do just that. His kingdom advanced and increased after this disaster. If he had gone into a state of despair and withdrawn, then perhaps his latter days would not have been as enriched and fruitful as they were. He refused to let the loss hold him back from moving forward. The appearance of defeat at the time of David's arrival in Ziklag was immediately before his greatest advancement and promotion. If you are in a place in life right now that seems as if everything is destroyed around you, it could very well be that your moment of greatest promotion is just around the corner.

David did not jump to conclusions concerning his plan of action when he became aware of the loss, but instead "David inquired of the Lord…" (1 Sam. 30:8a). It is important to wait on the Lord until you hear clearly how you are to proceed. In the midst of crisis it is easy to react rather than wait for the wisdom of the Lord. Often impulsive reactions will bring more failure.

This is what often happens with gamblers. They will have a few wins and then spiral into one loss after another after another. They keep thinking, "The next round will give me enough to get everything back." We know that the banks in casinos eventually get the return on everything. The reaction to the loss causes the gambler to play into the hand of more loss. The gambler then becomes controlled by loss. The root of the gambler's reaction was fear of loss, so in panic he (or she) hopes to get everything back by making impulsive decisions.

David did not respond to the devastation with a response that came from his own heart, but he inquired of the Lord and was given his marching orders on how to recover all. It is important to wait for clarity. Find that place of peace and rest in God's presence and wait for Him to speak the sure word of direction. (In this book, we do not cover the subject of "Hearing the Voice of God" but this is an important teaching that is found in my course called "The Prophetic Boot Camp" which is available on CD.)

Breaking Inner Vows

It is important to break the power of any inner vows you may have made as a result of unfulfilled or broken dreams. Inner vows are resolves or decisions made in our hearts. If these are made as a result of pain, they become landing strips for even more pain to enter our lives. They become self-inflicted curses.

I knew someone who was very hurt in a romantic relationship when she was around 18 years of age. Her heart was crushed. When the relationship was terminated, she vowed, "I will never give my heart to a man again!" This was an inner vow. By making this vow she unknowingly cursed herself with singleness even though she really did desire an intimate relationship.

In her mid-30s, she longed to be married, yet for almost twenty years she had not even been noticed by anyone of the opposite sex. While in prayer one day over the situation, she remembered the vow she made. She asked the Lord to forgive her and renounced the vow that day. Within a year, she was married. It is not difficult to break an inner vow. You simply ask the Lord to forgive you for making it and then renounce it in the name of Jesus. When you break an inner vow, you officially separate yourself from it. This is accomplished by calling the vow broken by faith. Sometimes it is helpful to record the breaking of a vow in a journal. Date the entry and call it official. You then have a point of reference for later should negative thoughts try to harass you.

Breaking Word Curses

As we outlined earlier, the words we speak create our course in life. Life and death are in the power of the tongue. In *Merriam-Webster's Online Dictionary*, one of the meanings of a *curse* is: "a cause of great harm or misfortune." James writes in James 3:9-10 that with our words we can curse people. You can actually bring great harm or misfortune to your life and to the lives of others by speaking negative words. We have the power to bless or to curse with our words.

The Bible has the final word and the true word about you. God has not called you to live a life of being cursed but of blessing. If you have lived a life of consistent mishap, injury, accident, misfortune, and harm, then it is possible that you are living under a curse. The good news is that curses can be broken!

Sometimes we curse ourselves with words. Every time you declare, "I am no good; nothing ever turns out for me; I am fat just like my grandmother—it runs in the family; I never have enough money; I am sick and tired; etc." you are actually landing a curse on yourself. The words you speak take on form and substance and have the ability to bring themselves to pass. Yikes! We need a crop failure here for sure. Many people have cursed themselves for years without knowing it, and then they wonder why everything goes wrong. These curses can be broken. Ask the Lord to forgive you for cursing yourself and others. Invite Him to cleanse your heart and life with His purifying blood. He will when you ask Him. Then begin to proclaim blessing after blessing. Make up for lost time! Bless others, too, and the blessings will come back on you.

The Lord has taught me to *only* receive blessing in my life. If something doesn't look like a blessing it must turn into one. Jesus has given us the power over all curses (see Luke 10:19). You are called to blessings and not curses. Put a stake in the ground of your life with that truth and settle the issue today—no more curses—only blessings! The more you proclaim blessing over yourself and others, the more blessings will manifest in your life. It is like planting seed in a garden. Whatever seed you plant will grow a harvest for you. You want a harvest of blessing.

The promises in the Word of God are the greatest source of blessing there is. I make it a practice to proclaim decrees of those promises over my life, family, ministry team, and partners every day. This sets me and those I love up for blessing. I also proclaim the decrees over the ministries and businesses God has entrusted to me. It works! The Word does not return void. The decrees in Appendix B of this book are some that I proclaim each day. We also have Decree CDs for both adults and children. I believe strongly in proclaiming blessing. The Word does not return void but accomplishes what it is sent to do.

We have discussed self-inflicted word curses, but others can proclaim word curses over us too. Sometimes, individuals are cursed by their parents or school teachers in their childhood. I have heard people testify that their parents told them they were stupid and wouldn't amount to anything. They believed it and lived under that curse until they were well into their adult life. It is possible for friends, family members, leaders, enemies, and peers to curse you without meaning to. It is through the negative words they decree over you. It would be glorious if everyone only spoke well of others, but unfortunately it is not that way on planet Earth yet. As a result, there is a whole lot of cursing going on.

I daily decree, "No weapon formed against me will succeed. In the name of Jesus, I silence every voice raised up to accuse me" (see Isaiah 54:17 NLT). Forgive those who speak evil against you and then proclaim blessings over your life. In the same way that light overpowers darkness, blessing overpowers cursing. Bless yourself each day—that will keep the curses away.

Building an Altar of Remembrance

When you have broken curses, forgiven anyone who has harmed you (even yourself), repented from any judgments you have made, and renounced any inner vows, then you can lay your broken, shattered, and unfulfilled dreams before the Lord. Give your broken dreams to Him in simple prayer. This becomes an altar.

An altar is a place of memorial or remembrance. It is a place of offering and sacrifice. Right now, you can decide to give all past dream failures and disappointments to God. That's right. You can place your disappointments and pain before Him as a sacrifice, an offering. Give them all to Him. He is bigger than all that has transpired. He is bigger than what you are facing now, and He can help you if you will surrender your disappointments.

Sometimes people think of an altar as being in a special location like a church, or made of materials such as stone or special wood. The altar we are talking about, however, is in the special location of the heart. The material that it is made of is a broken and contrite spirit that surrenders all the past failures and broken dreams to Him.

If you wish, you can make an altar right now by writing God a letter of surrender. Give Him all your dream failures. List them for Him. Release them to Him. He is with you and will receive your sacrifice as a gift. The following example may be of help to you:

Dear God,

I surrender the following disappointments, broken dreams, and failures to You (list them):

1. _____

2. _____

3. _____

4. _____

5. _____

I give them to You as a sacrifice. They are now Yours. Lord, please remove all the pain in my heart that I have suffered as a result of these disappointments. Forgive me for any bitterness or offense and help me to trust once again. Help me to dream again. Amen.

This is now a memorial, an altar of remembrance. You will probably want to date it. Whenever you feel disappointment knocking at the door of your emotions, remember this altar. Remember that you gave it all to God. It becomes a stake in the ground for you. It is now time to move on!

Get Specific About Your Dreams

The Bible says that "where there is no vision, the people perish" (Prov. 29:18 KJV). Fresh vision and thinking on life's possibilities will most likely fuel you with anticipation.

It is important to not only have a dream but to determine the details of your dream. For example, let's say that your desire is to purchase a home. That is a good vision, but you will want to ask yourself questions like, "What type of home do I desire? How big a home? Where is it located? Is it on a city lot, acreage, or in an apartment complex? What is the price range? What type of activities will take place there?" The more specific you are with the vision, the more tangible your dream will become in your heart.

I remember years ago when my husband and I launched into full-time preaching ministry and we no longer had a consistent monthly salary. We really needed a car at that time to get back and forth to meetings. I prayed one night in desperation, "Lord, I ask You for a small car that is good on gas."

The very next day while I was in my office the phone rang. The gentleman on the other end of the phone asked me if I had need of a car. He did not know about my situation or my prayer. I excitedly responded, "Yes, we do." He proceeded to explain how he had been in his devotion time that morning and felt he should call me and offer to give us a small car that he was not using any more. I was ecstatic! I asked him if it was good on gas and he said it was.

That weekend my husband and I went to pick up the car. It was definitely small and it was very good on gas, but it was a rust-bucket and did not run very well. We learned many lessons through that vehicle, but one for sure was to be very specific with our desires and prayers.

Write your dreams down so that you can meditate on them. This will bring more definition and clarity. Nebulous thoughts about what you would like to experience in life will not provide a landing strip for fulfillment. It is important to have your dreams clearly defined. Writing them down will help you in this process. In many studies and surveys it has been discovered that highly successful people have clearly defined visions that are written down. When you have clear vision, you will then be able to make goals and establish a plan of action to bring your dreams to fulfillment.

After you have your dreams clearly defined and written down, you will want to check through your dreams to make sure they are healthy. Remember, you were created by God for a life filled with blessings, and therefore He wants you to have good vision that will benefit you and others. Your dreams must not violate:

LOVE

PURITY

HUMILITY

HONESTY

WISDOM

INTEGRITY

GODLY MORALS AND CHARACTER

If you are not accustomed to believing for the dreams of your heart to come to pass, you may want to try working with one desire at a time. It is wise to begin with desires that you have faith to see accomplished and ones that will not take a long time to fulfill.

For example, it might be your dream to be a great mom and to raise children who will be an asset to society…and yes, even after 40 or even 50 this dream can be realized. All things are possible! This is a great desire to have, but it is probably going to take a number of years to see the fulfillment. It is also very general.

When you are just starting to realize your dreams, you may want to try something more specific that will take less time to fulfill. You can still move forward with the more long-term vision, but also have short-term dreams that can be realized. That way your faith and encouragement levels will keep growing. Try choosing something tangible that can be fulfilled in a shorter amount of time. The excitement of seeing the one dream fulfilled will produce the faith for the next and the next.

I remember a time when I desired new living room furniture. I looked through the stores and catalogues and found the type of furniture I was looking for. The vision was clear, specific, and something that could be fulfilled in a short amount of time (if I had a miracle—smile). I wrote down the vision of the furniture and even clipped out the pictures of the furniture.

I decided to give the existing furniture we had to someone in need. They had just moved into town and didn't have anything at all to furnish their rented apartment. Once we gave them the furniture, we were left with an empty living room. In my mind's eye, though, I could see the new furniture. I stood in that empty room and imagined the new furniture. I even wrote little notes that said: sofa, love seat, chair, coffee table, end table, etc., and set the papers down in the places where the furniture would sit once my dream was realized.

When people came to visit I invited them into the living room and asked, "How do you like my new furniture?" They looked at me with questioning eyes until I proceeded to take them on a tour of the living room describing the "new" furniture. It hadn't materialized yet. It was still only a dream...but at least it was a dream!

In less than a month, the real, tangible furniture was sitting in the place where the little notes and pictures had been. Eighteen months later we did the same thing again. We gave our furniture away and sat on "invisible dream furniture" for a couple of months until the tangible manifested. Dreaming and clarifying your desires is a key to living the Good Life.

Breaking the Cycle of Dream Failures

In the field of sports it is very important that a team does not experience too many losses in a row. After the third defeat, the morale of the team is affected and statistics prove that a pattern of defeat follows for the rest of the season. By the same principle it has been discovered that if a team wins three games in a row, they establish a pattern of victory.

As discussed earlier in this chapter, many people do not experience fulfillment in life because they have had one dream failure after another. They now live in a pattern of defeat and disappointment. It is important to change the pattern. If you begin with a desire that you are confident will be fulfilled, your success will most likely be assured. Break the defeat cycle and build a pattern of success, one fulfilled dream at a time. Once you get on a roll, it will take on a momentum of its own. It is important to break through to this place. You can do it!

You can change the course of your life through dreaming and seeing those desires fulfilled. When the smaller dreams are fulfilled then bigger ones will come easily. In fact, they won't even seem big any more.

Try Dreaming Right Now

In response, why don't you sit back and dream for a while? Find yourself a quiet place and relax. Tell every anxious thought to be silent. Think on things that are positive, good, and pleasant. Invite the Lord to fill you with His goodness and creativity. Ask Him to show you your potential. That's it. Just relax and bask in the glory of possibilities. This kind of thinking is healthy and will refresh you.

Now choose one desire that you would like to see realized in the next little while. Choose something that you believe can be accomplished within the next one to three months. Choose something practical and tangible for your first project. Remember that every dream realized will prepare the way for the next one.

Write your dream in a notebook or journal with as many specific details as you can. When you have a clear, well-defined dream, you are ready for the next step.

CHAPTER FOUR

On to Fulfillment

Importance of Goals

If you are going to fulfill the visions of your heart, then it is important to set some clear goals. Goals will enable you to put feet to your vision. Until goals are in place, your vision is only a vision. Your dream is only a dream. Goals will bring your dream from a place of nebulous bliss to practical application. Goals will provide a launching pad for a plan of action and your plan of action will enable your vision to become a reality.

Take a look at the dream you chose in the last lesson and think through it carefully. What goals do you want to accomplish through your vision? For example, if your vision is to purchase a home, it is helpful to solidify your goals and objectives for that home.

For years, my husband Ron and I commuted between our home and ministry office in Canada and a trailer in a Phoenix resort park where we lived during the winter months. As an itinerant conference speaker who does most of my traveling by air, it did not really matter which location I traveled from. We enjoyed the little one-bedroom trailer in Phoenix, but in time we established a ministry team there and brought on a full staff to accomplish increased assignments. All of a sudden we were crammed for space and needed a larger facility both for our lives and for the ministry office.

We began to dream. I decided to dream big. I envisioned a large home complete with guest rooms, personal office, swimming pool, and hot tub. The dream grew within our hearts and we set some goals:

1. Purchase a new home with all that we saw in our dream.
2. Use the home to facilitate ministry and hospitality for our team and others. Host team gatherings and guests, family, and friends in our home.
3. Use the home for a small production and ministry office.
4. Secure some commercial office space close to the home for our growing team and ministry operation.
5. Use the home for Bible studies and an internship program that we were launching.
6. Upgrade to enhance the quality and long-term investment of the home.

We now knew what our goals were. We were ready for a plan

of action to put it all into effect. We launched a plan of action based on the goals, and within nine months—with some faith and miracles—every goal was accomplished. We now live in the very home we dreamed about.

As a leader of a ministry it is my responsibility to not only receive vision and direction from the Lord, but to set goals to accomplish them. Recently our ministry received a vision to care for orphans in Africa. We had the dream, but we needed some goals in order to put some feet to the vision. Without goals your vision never become more than a vision.

One question to ask is, "What do you expect to accomplish?" With the orphans, we defined the goals clearly:

1. We initially set a goal to care for two homes of orphans in Mozambique. This included food, shelter, clothing, health needs, schooling, and caregiving for 40-80 children.
2. We set a goal to work through an existing Christian ministry that we were in relationship with. We would raise the finances and they would do the on-site labor.
3. We set our goal to raise $3,000 per month for the first six months and then another $3,000 per month after that (this would give us a total of four homes after the six months).
4. Our goal was to grow in compassion for the poor.
5. Our goal included the spreading of the vision to others who could also care for orphans.

6. Our goal involved creating an accounting infra-
    structure that could facilitate the support of many
    orphans and the building of children's homes.

7. Our goal included organizing those on our team
    who would visit and serve the orphans and the
    homes once we were established.

Once we had goals in place, we were ready to launch a plan of action to accomplish the goals that would fulfill the vision. I wrote the goals down and communicated them to our team along with the vision. Our team caught the vision, agreed with the goals, and our journey began. We are now supporting many orphans and many homes.

In the last chapter, you defined a specific dream in your heart. Now, write down the specific goals of your vision. What do you hope to accomplish through your vision? What specific things do you need in order to achieve it?

The Plan of Action

Your dreams will never be fulfilled without specific practicalities being put in place. Once your goals are well-defined and you know the purpose of your vision, then a plan of action is needed. Goals are what put feet to the vision; the plan of action gets those feet running. In the last section, I spoke about our personal dream to have a larger home and the goals of this project. In addition to defining both the dream and the goals, a plan of action was needed. What things need to be accomplished in order to see the goal fulfilled?

Sometimes it is good to determine your plan of action by asking questions. We asked questions like:

1. Do we need someone to help us find a home? Who?

2. Where do we want to live? What community? What subdivision?

3. What timing are we looking at?

4. What type of financing do we need and how do we secure it?

5. We then set some initial practicalities into place. I call it a To Do List:

   A. On March 3-4 we will seek the Lord as to which area of Phoenix we are to purchase in.

   B. On March 5, we will make an appointment with a real estate agent (our friend Sally) to discuss our desire for a new home. We will give her the specifics and ask her to show us some options that are already listed.

   C. On March 6, we will make an appointment with a loan officer to see what type of financing we qualify for.

   D. On March 7-9, we will look at options with the real estate agent.

   E. By March 10, we will make a choice and sign for a home to be built within 7-9 months.

As we prayed and sought the Lord for His wisdom, He directed our hearts to look for a home in the new community of Maricopa, Arizona. This town is less than half an hour from the Phoenix airport and only 20 minutes from a great shopping area in Chandler. There were many reasons that He gave us for relocating in Maricopa, but one of the sure words was in regard to the location He desired to establish our ministry center. *Maricopa* means "people drawn to the water." There was prophetic significance in this for us. In addition, Maricopa was a new, fast-growing community. Just 18 months prior, only 2,000 people were residing in Maricopa. At the time we were looking for our home, there were almost 20,000, and it was growing by 1,500 homes per month. This was a significant place to establish The Ministry Center, right in the foundations of a growing community.

Now that we knew the area, we contacted our real estate agent, who had been part of encouraging the move to Maricopa from an investment point of view. We made an appointment and she took us to view some options. We fell in love with one of the model homes and realized that it met all the goals that we had for the move. After checking out our financial qualifications and putting a plan of action into place for the raising of the down payment, we proceeded to purchase the home.

Our desire was to move in by October, but it was not until the end of December when we finally got the keys. Sometimes your timeline is not met as you hope, but it is better to have a goal for timing than not have a goal at all. Even if your goal is late in being met, at least it is realized. If you lack a goal and an appropriate plan of action, nothing will happen, and years later you will think back to your good idea and say, "We should have moved on that vision when we had it. We thought about it but didn't act on it." And you know what? You will probably be sitting in the same position where you were years previously. Most likely you will not have progressed.

It takes a clear dream, some well-defined goals, and a prayerfully thought-through plan of action in order to fulfill a dream. Once you have your plan of action, then for goodness sake, *act!* Don't just think about it for five years, but *act.* Usually, it is better to act sooner than later. Your good thoughts and intentions will not fulfill your dreams. It takes action.

I believe that *whatever you vividly dream with God, passionately desire, and act on in fervent faith, shall surely come to pass.*

Take some time to prayerfully think through the plan of action to accomplish your goals. Write them out. Put a check mark beside each one as you accomplish them.

Success Factor

I have noticed that some folks like to plunge in to a large dream before they have learned to accomplish the smaller ones. In most cases this does not work. You need to build the *success factor* into your life through the accomplishment of one vision at a time and one level at a time. Your faithfulness in the stewardship and success of the small visions will lead you into the next level, and then your faithfulness and success on that level will lead you to the next and the next.

I can always tell when I am being challenged to another level. Each level is met with challenges that have to be overcome.

Persistence is necessary. In every new level you will usually find faith tests as well as love tests that need to be passed in order to attain the success factor on that level. The fulfillment of your larger dreams will be realized through your faithfulness and fruitfulness in the smaller ones.

This is why it is good to have long-term and short-term goals. It is healthy to dream big. It is important to do so. But make sure that you have shorter-term goals to accomplish on the way.

As you overcome each challenge with faith, persistence, and love, you will gain stronger measures of fruitfulness and accomplishment. These increased measures of accomplishment will work for you as you enter your next level. This is what I call the *success factor*.

For example, your big dream might be to be a brain surgeon. This is a fantastic vision (yes, even in your 50s—why not?). It is important, however, to live within smaller dreams on your way to the larger one. You don't just show up in an operating theater and start performing brain surgery. If becoming a brain surgeon is your dream, then begin by getting the academic grades that will give entrance into college and medical school. This will be your first dream and goal to accomplish.

Define the vision and write down your goals and your plan of action. Then act on it. Go for the A to A-plus average in your entrance level academic training. Work toward that until you accomplish it. Overcome the obstacles and the testing periods in that season. When you accomplish that dream, you will have faith to move to the next one. The success factor will move with you. The next dream might be to gain entrance into a good medical school.

Determine your goals and plan of action carefully and prayerfully. Persevere until you attain each one. Each fulfilled vision will strengthen the success factor and prepare you for the next.

Eventually, if you continue to move forward, you will find yourself in that operating theater that you dreamed about years before. How did you get there? One fulfilled dream at a time.

Always celebrate the tests and trials in each season. It is the endurance and perseverance you walk in during those tests that builds the success factor in you. The bigger the tests, the bigger the victories.

No Quick Fix—Take Your Time

Sometimes individuals want to recover losses quickly. An individual I know personally experienced a wonderful measure of overnight success in investments at a young age. Within a year, however, he made an investment that produced unpredicted and significant losses. Overnight he lost everything. He had borrowed money from financial institutions and friends. He had also mortgaged his home to the maximum equity allowance in order to make an investment into the "opportunity of a lifetime." Through this devastating mishap, an unhealthy pattern to produce recovery of losses entered his life. He was determined to make the loss back for his devastated friends as well as for himself and his family. As a result he borrowed more money at high interest rates, as well as through acquaintances who trusted him. He took the borrowed money and invested it into risky, high-percentage, quick-return stocks. The stocks bottomed out and once again he lost everything.

If he had taken his time to rebuild slowly after the first loss, he could have built up his equity again in time. Once you establish a pattern of success, even if it is small at first, it becomes your portion in life. Once you establish it carefully over time, you will always be able to build back to that level even if you have a tragedy along the way.

Unfortunately, the same principle seems to work with failures. If you have a pattern of failure in your life, then you will live in that pattern until it is broken. It is best to break it with one little victory at a time. Build the success factor in your life by accomplishing at least one success every day. Make small daily goals and then accomplish them. Celebrate the success. Set new goals the next day and accomplish them. Through this deliberate pattern of walking successfully in fulfilled goals, you will build the success factor into your life. Very seldom will you find success sustained through quick, overnight successes.

The success factor, which is the long-term progressive pattern of fruitfulness, is only secured through the passing of tests on each level. When that part of the process is missing, there is nothing to sustain long-term success. It is proven statistically that people who win large amounts of money in lotteries most of the time fall back into old patterns very quickly. This is due to the fact that they do not have the success factor built into that level of financial gain. They drop back to the last place where they passed their tests.

If you have had a life of failure, stuck in a rut, and spinning wheels, then walk out of the rut. Leave the failure behind and start all over. If you continue to do the things you have always done, you will continue to get the same results as always. Start from basic foundations. Begin with simple daily goals that are easy to accomplish. God can make all things new. Bury the humiliation, failure, and shame of past failures in His love and grace. Out of death can spring life. God can make all things new if you are willing to start afresh. Don't try to get everything back over night. As we grow older, sometimes that panic rises within us and causes us to make unwise choices. Take it slowly—there is still time. Even if you are 80 or 90 years of age, there is still time to build the success factor into your life. How much more if you are in your 40s or 50s?

Learn from the past. As I mentioned in a previous chapter, carefully and intentionally identify the things that caused the failures, and then don't step back into the same pattern again. Sometimes your friends and family can see things more clearly. Ask for their input and seek out some mature counsel. Find those you can be accountable to so that you don't walk the same way again.

It is never too late to change patterns of failure and build the success factor into your life. Why not start today?

CHAPTER FIVE

Faith

The second half of life is full of opportunity and potential. There is nothing too hard for the Lord. All things are possible if you only believe! This means that your opportunities to experience fullness are limitless!

I have personally enjoyed a journey of faith since 1976. After I accepted Jesus as my Savior, I read the Bible and discovered promise after promise. All the promises in the Word are for every child of His. As a young Christian, I read in First John 5:14-15, "…if we ask anything according to His will, He hears us. And if we know that He hears us in whatever we ask, we know that we have the requests which we have asked from Him." I also read the words of Jesus in Mark 11:24, "Therefore I say to you, all things for which you pray and ask, believe that you have received them, and they will be granted you."

I was completely undone at the discovery of these promises. Not only had I been completely forgiven of all my sins and given a brand new life in Christ, He had also promised to answer all my prayers. I simply needed to align my desires with His. Wow! I put these promises into practice right away with child-like faith.

I quickly discovered that the Lord wanted to be intimately involved with everything that was important to me. I prayed for my family's salvation. They are now all born again. I prayed for my neighbor's son to be healed from a colon disorder, and he was miraculously healed. I prayed that I would get a job that I wasn't qualified for—for which over 120 people applied—and I got it! I prayed for a parking spot in front of the bank as the street was congested with traffic. The next time around the block, a car pulled out of the spot right in front of the door to the bank just in time for me to drive into my prayed-for spot. When guests came over unexpectedly, I prayed for multiplication of food at the dinner table and saw miraculous provision right before my eyes. These prayers and numerous others were all prayed during my first week of becoming a Christian. I was rattling off prayers like a machine gun rattles off rounds of ammunition...and many of the answers manifested within minutes of my requests.

Well, that was the beginning of my journey of faith. I love living by faith! My husband and I actually have no other means of support. We believe for everything. Being in ministry, we are always invited by the Lord to believe for things to manifest that we have absolutely no power in ourselves to accomplish. The more impossible it looks, the better we like it—we then see the raw power and glory of God bring it all to pass. I love it!

This invitation to believe God does not stop when you turn 40. In fact, for many the life of faith is only beginning…and it gets better and better. I am going to believe for God to perform His exploits until I breathe my last breath. I will probably pray, "Just one more prayer, Lord…"

God responds to faith and not to need. There are many needs in the world, and yet we do not see them all met. God responds to faith. He is looking for someone to believe so that He can move. The Bible says that the heavens belong to the Lord, but the earth He has given to the sons of men (see Ps. 115:16). God has given the dominion of the earth to those in Christ. Dare to believe Him to do great things for you and through you.

I love meeting folks who have retired from secular employment and have not let the grass grow under their feet. Often we fail to see the significance of our ministry before the Lord within the secular arena, but even worse is to see the wisdom of those in the second half of life lie buried in a life of retirement. I actually don't believe that we should ever retire. We should just go from glory to glory and from one experience in God to the next, whether that is in a secular field or not.

I meet people everywhere in post-retirement from secular fields who are making their lives count. They are so cool! I once met a couple who left a medical practice and now lead teams of medical students every year to the mission field. The rest of the year they volunteer in their local church. In the winter they join a motor home group who travel around the nation from campsite to campsite sharing the gospel. They are having the time of their lives.

Another couple I met had owned a business that consumed most of their time and focus. At 63 years of age they got born again. At 65 years of age they were filled with the Spirit and learned that the healing ministry was for today. At 67 years of age the husband decided to sell his life-long business and launch out in a healing ministry. He believed for the sick to be healed and was used powerfully to release supernatural miracles to those who were afflicted

Gwen Shaw, president and founder of End Time Handmaidens, is in her 70s and is a burning torch for Jesus as she believes for His glory to spread like fire in the earth. She always has fresh vision that requires faith.

Dr. C. Peter Wagner launched his world-renowned Wagner Leadership Institute at an age when most Americans live in retirement. Today thousands of people are being blessed as a result. He simply took a step of faith as he refused to be inactive with what was in his hand to give. Many ministers retire from their pastorates in their 50s and 60s and then dry up. Dr. Wagner has kept his faith alive and active. He is a fruitful vine in the second half of life!

Freda Lindsay with Christ For The Nations is another "go-getter" in her second half of life. After her husband passed away she continued to lead the vision and fueled the mandate with her faith. She kept herself fresh and invigorated by activating her faith on a daily basis.

What Is Faith?

In Hebrews 11:1 (KJV) the Bible describes *faith* as being "the substance of things hoped for, the evidence of things not seen."

In Mark 9:23, Jesus said, "All things are possible to him who believes."

Faith is a powerful force that makes your dreams a reality. True faith is not based on man's ability but on God's. Without God, we have nothing. Every good and perfect gift comes from Him (see James 1:17). Without God's glorious grace in our life we have nothing. Every good and perfect thing that people enjoy in life comes from Him, including our faith.

Many operate in the faith that God gives every individual but they do not honor Him or thank Him. It is important to acknowledge where our faith comes from. There are various types of faith, but all faith is given by God. There is the natural faith that every person has. This is why every person has the ability to believe. There is also a holy faith that is given to those who are believers in Christ. This is the same faith that Jesus operated in when He walked the earth. This is the faith that allows us to walk in the supernatural and miraculous realm. This is the type of faith that grants us the guarantee of an abundant life if we exercise it. Every Christian receives this special faith when they ask Jesus to come into their lives as their personal Savior and Lord.

Just because you have this faith doesn't mean it automatically works for you. In order for this faith to produce results, you have to use it. This faith comes from relationship with God. It first enters us when we invite Him to come into our hearts, and following that experience it grows through our devotion times with Him. The Bible says, "Faith comes from hearing, and hearing by the word of Christ" (Rom. 10:17). Your faith will grow as you spend time in worship, Bible reading, fellowship, and prayer.

When Jesus died on the cross, He gave every blessing in heaven and earth to those who believed in Him. In Ephesians 1:3 the Bible says, "Blessed be the God and Father of our Lord Jesus Christ, who has blessed us with every spiritual blessing in the heavenly places in Christ." In Second Peter 1:3 (KJV), the Scriptures teach that His divine power has "given unto us all things that pertain unto life and godliness...." Everything is every thing! That means we can believe big! There is nothing that has been withheld from us. Whatever we need to live in fullness in our second half of life has already been granted to us in Christ.

Faith is the connector that takes the invisible promise and makes it a reality in our experience. Remember, "All things are possible if you believe." Some people do not experience abundant, full, and overflowing life because of negative thoughts. They believe that life is always hard for them and that nothing turns out right. Because they believe this, they receive it. You will receive what you believe for, whether good or bad. Faith is a powerful force.

Faith is dependent on your thoughts. It is important to make sure that your thoughts line up with the promises and will of God. His nature is pure, loving, and kind. When you think about your dreams, goals, and desires, ask yourself if these things are healthy for you and others. Examine your dreams and see if they line up with God's desires. For example, let's say that one of your dreams is to help fatherless children. As a result of this dream you set a goal to become a "Big Brother" to a young boy without a father. Your plan of action involves applying to the Big Brother organization, awaiting acceptance, and being assigned a child. Is this dream, goal, and plan of action in line with God's desires? If so, you can activate your faith toward the accomplishment of this goal and trust God for favor and a successful assignment. Whatever you need to accomplish that desire will be granted when your thoughts line up with God's.

The Bible says that God will not withhold any good thing from those who walk uprightly. He wants to give you good things. He wants to give you fullness in the second half of life. Believe Him to give you the desires of your heart. He has called you to live in the blessing realm all the days of your life...only believe!

The Enemies: Doubt and Unbelief

Doubt and unbelief are negative forces that can destroy your life. These two enemies will keep you from experiencing fullness. They kept the Israelites from experiencing the Promised Land in the Bible. God had given them promises when they were in Egypt but they constantly doubted Him and His promises. As a result they were stuck out in the wilderness for 40 years. Many people today are stuck in the wilderness of lack and unfulfilled dreams because they doubt God.

The Israelites were full of faith when the Red Sea parted allowing them to pass to the other side in safety. They were full of faith as they watched their enemies swallowed up in the waves behind them. But that faith was short-lived. As soon as a trial came, they lost their focus and their faith was nowhere to be found.

You will discover if you have faith or not during trials and testing periods. Are you a believer or a doubter? Sometimes people are afraid to believe because they have been disappointed in the past. We don't always understand why things turn out the way they do, but we need to keep faith nonetheless as God's ways are higher than ours. Faith pleases Him and faith accomplishes things. It is always best to believe even if things don't turn out the way you envisioned at first. You will receive insight at some point—and then everything will make sense. In the meantime continue to believe. It is healthier. A life of unbelief and doubt is a life that is in danger of bitter sadness and oppression. An unbelieving skeptic exudes negativity and oppression, while a faith-filled individual exudes hope and optimism. Which one would you rather be around?

Determine today to be a person who believes instead of doubts. Perhaps you were a "believer" in your earlier years but as you grew older you suffered disappointments and lost your faith. Doubt, skepticism, and negativity set in. I ask you, has it made you happier to live in doubt, unbelief, and pessimism? Have these mind-sets worked to give you a good life? I say not.

Finish the last laps of your years in strength, a positive outlook, and joy. Take up that shield of faith today and run your race with endurance. There is so much waiting for you. Dare to believe again and watch God pour out blessings upon you. Be a believer and not a doubter...for the rest of your days.

CHAPTER SIX

The Key Principle

There is one Kingdom principle that I believe is the granddaddy of them all. I live my life by this principle and will often tell people that if they were to choose only one of God's wonderful Kingdom laws to live by, this would be the one to choose. This principle is especially important to live by in the second half of life. It is the law of sowing and reaping.

The law of gravity is a God-created law. What goes up, comes down. This law works for all the people, all the time. Why? It is because it is a God-created law. God-created laws work for all the people all the time. I can tell you through over 30 years of tested experience that the law of sowing and reaping works, works, works! It has never failed me once.

Wise people live inside the boundaries of the laws God created and established. There are natural laws, spiritual laws, and moral laws that we find outlined in the Bible. If you respect the laws, you will benefit, and if you violate the laws, you will suffer. It is that simple! Using the simple example of the law of gravity, it is easy to demonstrate both the blessing of this law and the negative consequence you would suffer if you violated it. The blessing of this law is obvious: our feet are anchored to the earth. I am so thankful that I don't live my life floating around in outer space somewhere. One negative consequence due to violation of this law could look like this: I decide to walk off a cliff to get to the other side of the Grand Canyon (after all, it is a much shorter distance than going all the way around via the highway). I don't need to describe this consequence to you; simply let your imagination paint the details!

The Law of Sowing and Reaping

In the very beginning when God created man, He blessed us and said, "Be fruitful and multiply" (Gen. 1:28). This is our portion. In order to be fruitful, you must plant seed. In Genesis 8:22, the Lord made a promise to Noah that is still true to this day: "While the earth remains, seedtime and harvest, and cold and heat, and summer and winter, and day and night shall not cease."

The earth remains even as you are reading this book. If the earth remains, there is seedtime and a corresponding harvest. This is a law. When you plant the seed, it will grow and produce a harvest. Your harvest will not be unto addition but unto multiplication. When you plant a bean seed in the ground, it doesn't give you one or two beans but many. The seed sown is multiplied and each bean on the plant contains more seed as well. A wise farmer enjoys eating and marketing his crop as well as collecting the multiplied seed in order to grow more. It is unwise for him to eat all the seed. He must continue to sow in order to reap.

Second Corinthians 9:6-10 says this:

> *Now this I say, he who sows sparingly will also reap sparingly, and he who sows bountifully will also reap bountifully. Each one must do just as he has purposed in his heart, not grudgingly or under compulsion, for God loves a cheerful giver. And God is able to make all grace abound to you, so that always having all suffi-ciency in everything, you may have an abundance for every good deed; As it is written, He scattered abroad, He gave to the poor, His righteousness endures forever. Now He who supplies seed to the sower and bread for food will supply and multiply your seed for sowing and increase the harvest of your righteousness.*

The law of sowing and reaping cannot fail and it will not fail. It is a spiritual law. Let's look at a few key points found in this passage.

1. You will reap in proportion to what you sow. If you sow only a little, you will reap only a little. If you sow much, you will reap much. What will happen if you sow nothing?

2. Your sowing must be from a desire and conviction of the heart if you are going to reap the results. Your cheerfulness, conviction, and expectation in sowing launches this law into action.

3. God's grace (His divine influence upon your life and His favor toward you) will give you everything you need to sow. He will give you your seed. If you don't have seed to sow, then ask Him for it. He will give it to you.

4. God will cause the seed that you sow to multiply. This multiplication is found in the fruit of the seed sown as well as in the seed for sowing. That means you will have more than enough to be filled yourself and enough to grow a greater crop the next time you sow.

Types of Seed

Second Corinthians 9:6-10 isn't referring only to the seed you sow in a vegetable garden and neither is it limited to the context of financial offerings that it was written in. The law includes "whatever" we sow. If I want beans, then I had better sow bean seeds. If I sow corn seeds I will not reap beans.

If I want friends, I don't need to sow potatoes in my garden of life. I need to sow friendship into the lives of people. A couple in a church approached me full of dismay one Sunday after the morning service. They said, "We have been in this church for over six months now and no one has invited us over for lunch or asked us out." I expressed my sadness over this situation but asked them a question, "How many people have *you* invited over to your home for lunch?" They were a little shocked at my response and honestly responded. They explained that they didn't believe they needed to reach out to others because people should be inviting them. I shared about the law of sowing and reaping. It wasn't nice that they had been neglected as newcomers in the church they attended, but they could turn the whole situation around through operating in this one key law. I suggested that they begin sowing into their desire for relationships in their new church home.

The next Sunday, they invited two families over to their home for lunch. Every Sunday after that, they made it their habit to have people over. A number of months later when I happened to see them, they ran up and shared the good news with me. "We are having the time of our lives," they exclaimed. "We have been meeting so many people and have started a hospitality ministry in our church." They eventually became the overseers of the Newcomers Ministry and then were invited to lead a cell group and eventually to church elder- ship. They became one of the most popular couples in the church.

This great victory came about through exercising the law of sowing and reaping. They planted the seeds of hospitality and friendship and they reaped a huge harvest. For the first six months, no one had invited them for lunch, or anything else for that matter, but they found personal fulfillment in blessing others. So much so, that they didn't even mind not being reached out to by others. Eventually, however, the return of the seed sown pro- duced a massive, ongoing harvest that lasted their entire lives. The law of sowing and reaping will launch anyone into a full and abundant life.

There are many types of seed. Here is another example. As a new Christian, I loved the Word of God. Every day when I read the Scriptures, I came alive through the quickening of a passage or two. I got so excited about the fresh revelation that I shared it with everyone who would listen. I called friends on the phone who were also hungry to know the ways of God more. If anyone dropped in for coffee, they would get a free download. God gave me the seed, which in this case was the revelation of the Word. I was sowing it through sharing the revelation with others. The more revelation I shared, the more revelation I received. Eventually, I was invited to teach Bible studies and then preach in churches, conferences, and seminars. Later, I sowed the Word through tapes, CDs, manuals, and books, and now through television, radio, and the Internet. In the beginning I sowed a few small seeds in a small sphere of influence. Now the seed of revelation has been multiplied and the sphere of influence has been increased to the nations of the world. This is the law of sowing and reaping. If you desire more revelation of the Word, then sow the revelation you now have into the lives of others.

Financial Abundance

The key to living in abundance in the financial arena of life is again found in the law of sowing and reaping. If you want finances, you sow finances. If you want a new car, then sow a car. If you desire new furniture or clothes, then sow furniture and clothing. This is the key to fruitfulness. We have been made in the image of God, and He is a giver. He gives extravagantly! He gave the very best of

Himself. He gave His only begotten Son so that the whole earth could be blessed with eternal life. Luke 6:38 (KJV) teaches us:

> Give, and it shall be given unto you; good measure, pressed down, and shaken together, and running over, shall men give into your bosom. For with the same measure that ye mete withal it shall be measured to you again.

Good Soil

When you are sowing, you need to be aware of the soil. When seed is planted into good soil, it will grow well. In Mark 4:1-20, Jesus teaches His disciples a parable about a sower and his seed. He makes it clear in the parable that it is important to sow in good ground, otherwise your seed is wasted. The following are the four types of ground Jesus described in His parables:

1. Some seed was sown by the side of the road where the birds came and ate it.
2. Some seed was sown on rocky soil and was unable to take root.
3. Some seed was sown amongst thorns and got choked out.
4. Some seed was sown in good soil and yielded 30-, 60-, and 100-fold returns.

It is obvious for those of us who long to live a rich, full life that the soil yielding 30-, 60-, and 100-fold is the type of soil we want to sow in. We do not want to waste our seed by throwing it on the side of the road, planting it in rocky ground, or sowing it amongst thorns and weeds.

When I sow the Word of God into the ground of a hungry heart I will yield the greatest return. In my younger years I was full of enthusiasm about Jesus. I would tell everyone how wonderful He was. Some just kept walking by and not giving an ear to it at all. Others were hardened in their heart and very argumentative. Others were interested but were caught up in the standards and cares of the world, so the Word never took root in them. There were others, however, who were ripe and hungry for all that God had for them. They received the seed and it grew in them. Some of them became faithful members of local churches and others full-time preachers of the gospel. The seed that fell into the good soil yielded 30-, 60-, and 100-fold returns.

This is not to say that the seed sown into poor soil will never grow. Sometimes it will sprout up years later. But it does determine how much time I spend sowing into a life. I learned the hard way that my time and energy gets wasted if I sow into those who are not ready. It is best to find the hungry and invest seed into their lives. Those whose soil is ready will yield a great return.

I am an itinerant speaker. The subjects I teach are loved by some and despised by others. Where then should I sow my seed? It is wise to sow in ground that is ready to receive the seed. Sowing into this rich, fertile ground brings forth a great harvest.

Expect a Harvest

Do you know a farmer who does not expect a harvest when he plants his seed? This would be a strange mind-set. Imagine a farmer going out on his field saying, "Oh, how I love casting this seed into the ground. Yes, it gives me great pleasure. I don't care about the harvest though. It makes no difference to me if I reap or not—I simply sow for the sheer enjoyment of it!" You would think this individual was ready for some serious counseling, wouldn't you? Well, sometimes people who sow things in life do so in faith but without an expectation of reaping. They sow friendship, finances, God-given gifting, and acts of kindness without any expectation of return.

It is good to have a generous heart. It is good to give without selfish desires or manipulation, but it is also important to know that when you sow, reaping is involved. One of my God-given gifts is communication. I engage in this through speaking, writing, television, radio, Internet, Web video, DVD production, and sometimes through dramatizing messages. When I sow into people's lives I expect to see fruit. I might never know what that fruit is in their lives—as sometimes I don't have the privilege of meeting them—but I *believe* for fruitfulness in their lives as a result of the seed sown. I trust that their lives will be richer, fuller, and increased in blessing because of the message I sow into their lives. Their personal blessing is as a result of the seed sown and is part of the harvest. The other part of the harvest involves my ability to receive and deliver more life-giving messages to increased numbers of people. I expect this. When I am faithful to sow the gift into others, it should increase in fruitfulness and in its sphere of influence.

In the area of finances, Ron and I always make sure we sow into good ground. We look for ground that is well-tilled and fruitful. Our heart is to see people blessed with the gospel, so we sow into works and ministries that are fruitful in this arena. When we sow into good ground we reap more finances in return *and* share in the eternal fruit and reward of their ministries.

My youngest son and his wife have their own company in the building industry. When they first got married, they sowed generous offerings into our ministry because they knew it was good ground. Our ministry is also in the "building industry," although in a different context. We build the advancement of God's love and grace in the earth. They sowed in faith and believed to reap back. They sowed finance and they believed to reap finance. They did! Year after year, they increased in both financial blessing and in fruitfulness. Every year, their company grew in profitability and in favor. They sowed with an expectation to reap. They sowed bountifully and they reaped bountifully. They sowed into good soil—soil that was producing fruit. They sowed into a ministry that was involved in "building" and they received a building grace that enabled them to be successful in the building industry.

We have had folks sow into our ministry on a regular basis because it is a prophetic ministry. Several have testified concerning their personal growth in the prophetic after they began sowing on a regular basis. They sowed with an expectation. Others sow into our ministry because our soil produces fruitfulness in the area of evangelism and media. They reap with intentional faith because they sow with a vision to reap. Many of the Breaker Team financial partners in our ministry testify regularly of the financial and spiritual breakthroughs and miracles that have come as a result of sowing into good ground.

Our ministry sows into many other ministries. For me, more is better! I find fruitful ministries in the area of evangelism, the prophetic, supernatural signs and wonders, mercy and justice, and media, and sow good seed into good ground with an expectation of a harvest. In faith, I claim a return on the harvest, but also on the area of anointing I am sowing into. I love this and constantly see the results! The more I sow, the bigger the harvest.

Deliverance From the Withholding Spirit

One of the greatest enemies to the law of sowing and reaping is a withholding spirit. This spirit usually finds a landing strip through fear, and it is common to see this spirit grip those in the second half of life. Some folks are afraid to sow in their second half of life because they believe if they do they will not have anything left. I have heard them say, "I am on a limited income." Well, that is probably why—they are given over to a withholding spirit as their scope of vision is so small. In God, there are no limits. Life in God is not like a pie that only has so many pieces, and when they are all eaten, it is gone. We cannot and must not live by that mind-set.

If you truly believe that the law of sowing and reaping is true, then it is more important to sow in your second half of life if you want abundance in your latter days. Sow in order to reap.

Your latter days are to be greater than the former—in every way. Sow unto this end.

If a farmer hoarded his seed and said, "I only have one bag of seed and it has to last me five years," he would be wise to take a pile of that seed and sow it into some good ground—the sooner, the better. As he does, that will provide more food and more seed in the coming season. When he replants from the seed harvest in that season, it will produce more again, and in five years he will have exponential amounts of food. If he hoards and does not plant it, he surely will need to be careful how much seed he eats. If he eats very carefully, then maybe he can make it stretch for the five years…but man, what a terrible way to live! And what happens after the five years?

This is the opposite thinking and action to the law of sowing and reaping. In the Bible you find many stories where even in times of hardship, if God's people sowed, they reaped. Isaac, for example, sowed in a time of famine, and within a year he reaped 100-fold as the Lord blessed him (see Gen. 26:12).

A small lunch was sown one day on the hillside where Jesus was teaching. Five thousand people were fed and a harvest of 12 baskets appeared *after* everyone had all they wanted. They began this catering experience with only five loaves and two fish. It is a good thing that someone did not withhold their lunch that day. Their sacrifice not only fed the multitude but they received a whole lot more in return.

If what you have is too small to meet your need, then it is probably seed. Don't eat your seed but sow it. In First Kings 17, Elijah went to Zeraphath in the midst of a famine. He asked a widow to get him some water and bread. In verses 12-16 (KJV), we find her response:

> And she said, As the Lord thy God liveth, I have not a cake, but an handful of meal in a barrel, and a little oil in a cruse: and, behold, I am gathering two sticks, that I may go in and dress it for me and my son, that we may eat it, and die. And Elijah said unto her, Fear not; go and do as you have said: but make me thereof a little cake first, and bring it unto me, and after make for thee and for thy son. For thus saith the Lord God of Israel, The barrel of meal shall not waste, neither shall the cruse of oil fail, until the day that the Lord sendeth rain upon the earth. And she went and did according to the saying of Elijah: and she, and he, and her house, did eat many days. And the barrel of meal wasted not, neither did the cruse of oil fail, according to the word of the Lord, which he spake by Elijah.

It would have been easy for this dear woman to withhold the final little bit of meal and oil that she had, but she was willing to sow it. When she did, she kicked into a new dimension—a miraculous one. What she had was not enough to meet her need so it became her seed. When she sowed her only seed, she and her son were sustained through the famine.

When my husband and I experienced lean times, we never stopped sowing. We stood on the promises of the Word of God and believed in the law of sowing and reaping. Sometimes we did not reap right away, but years later, it came back on every wave.

Flowing

In a pond, it is important to keep the water flowing in and flowing out. If the flow stops, the pond becomes stagnant. In the second half of life, many dam up their ponds and they become stagnant. Nothing much can live in a stagnant pond. Keep a good amount of your life, giftings, and finance flowing out so that more can flow in. This is how you will stay fresh. Look for ways even right now that you can have things flow out of your life to the world around you.

In the parable of the talents, Jesus tells about two who invested their talents and received reward in return and one who withheld and received judgment.

Matthew 25:14-30:

> *"For it is just like a man about to go on a journey, who called his own slaves and entrusted his possessions to them. To one he gave five talents, to another, two, and to another, one, each according to his own ability; and he went on his journey. Immediately the one who had received the five talents went and traded with them, and gained five more talents. In the same manner the one who had received the two talents gained two more. But he who received the one talent went away, and dug a hole in the ground and hid his master's money. Now after a long time the master of those slaves came and settled accounts with them. The one who had received the five talents came up and brought five more talents,*

saying, 'Master, you entrusted five talents to me. See, I have gained five more talents.' His master said to him, 'Well done, good and faithful slave. You were faithful with a few things, I will put you in charge of many things; enter into the joy of your master.' Also the one who had received the two talents came up and said, 'Master, you entrusted two talents to me. See, I have gained two more talents.' His master said to him, 'Well done, good and faithful slave. You were faithful with a few things, I will put you in charge of many things; enter into the joy of your master.' And the one also who had received the one talent came up and said, 'Master, I knew you to be a hard man, reaping where you did not sow and gathering where you scattered no seed. And I was afraid, and went away and hid your talent in the ground. See, you have what is yours.' But his master answered and said to him, 'You wicked, lazy slave, you knew that I reap where I did not sow and gather where I scattered no seed. Then you ought to have put my money in the bank, and on my arrival I would have received my money back with interest. Therefore take away the talent from him, and give it to the one who has the ten talents.' For to everyone who has, more shall be given, and he will have an abundance; but from the one who does not have, even what he does have shall be taken away. Throw out the worthless slave into the outer darkness; in that place there will be weeping and gnashing of teeth."

Sometimes people experience darkness and agony in their second half of life because they failed to allow their gifts to flow to others. You will always receive a return on what you invest in faith. There is no time like now to begin to let the "river flow."

Wisdom

We need to have wisdom in the area of sowing and reaping. Wisdom is given to every person who lacks it and asks God for it (see James 1:5). In wisdom's right hand is length of days and in her left hand is honor and riches (see Prov. 3:16). Ask in faith for the wisdom you need and wait on the Lord for the entrance of wisdom that teaches how to sow, what to sow, where to sow, and when and how to reap.

Wisdom not only teaches you how to invest your finances and talents but also how to maintain them. Wisdom is a principal thing, available to all who desire it. I love wisdom and will often read the first ten chapters of Proverbs which give keys on how to grow in wisdom. If you love and honor wisdom, you will get filled with it.

Crop Failures

The law of sowing and reaping works not only for good seed sown but also for bad seed. If you sow discord, you will reap discord. If you steal, you will be stolen from. If you dishonor others, you will be dishonored. If you withhold from others in their time of need, you will be withheld from blessing in your time of need. If you sow judgment and criticism, you will reap it. It is the law! This law works for all the people all the time with good seed or bad seed.

It is important to have clean soil in which to sow good seed. How then do we get rid of the crop that has grown from the bad seeds planted in the past? This is easy—*ask for a crop failure.* Admit your mistakes and ask God to forgive you for planting bad seeds in your own life or in the lives of others. Name them one by one, if you can, and ask for forgiveness. Forgive others who may have sown bad seed into your life. Then ask God to cleanse the field of your life from the bad crops that have sprung up form the bad seed. He will. He loves to do this for you.

When the field is clean, then plant lots of good seeds. Each day, ask God to forgive you for any bad seed that you may have planted in your life or in the lives of anyone else. Keep the garden weeded!

Prayer for Crop Failure

Dear Heavenly Father,

I am deeply sorry for planting negative seeds in my life and in the lives of others. I ask You to forgive me for each and every one of them. I ask You for a crop failure of every destructive and negative seed that I have ever planted. Cause the soil of my life to be fertile and ready for good seed. I pray for good seeds to be sown in the lives of those where I have planted bad seed in the past.

Thank You, Father, for answering my prayer.

Amen.

Sow Good Seed for the Fulfillment of Desires

Now that you have nice clean soil to plant in, think of what specific kind of crop you would like to reap. Once you define this, then sow into those areas proportionately. Remember, your harvest is always bigger than your seed. Sow bountifully.

I will give you an example:

DESIRED CROP: To receive favor

Seeds to Sow:

- Sow prayers each day, asking for favor to increase in my life.
- Make daily Scripture decrees over my life for favor.
- Write a daily encouraging note to someone expressing favor.
- Once a week sow a gift into someone's life to express favor.
- Each day, remember to esteem, prefer, and favor others more than myself.

HARVEST: Answers to prayers.

- Word decrees come into manifestation.
- Receive encouraging notes from others expressing favor.
- Receive gifts that express favor.
- Others will esteem me higher than themselves.
- Others will prefer me before themselves.

Now, make your personal list:

Description of Desire	Description of Seed

Journal the Harvest

Review your seed list above from time to time and see if you have produced a harvest. Speak blessing over your seed and the ground it is planted in. I usually speak something like this: "In Jesus' name, I bless the seed I have planted and I bless the soil it is in. I pray for a 100-fold return." This is how you can water your seed. When your harvest manifests, then journal that and thank the Lord for His goodness. Praise Him.

Date	Description of Harvest

CHAPTER SEVEN

Health, Fitness, and Beauty

I think that one of the greatest fears in the second half of life is not having the health and strength to live a quality, strong, and vibrant existence. Aging is a natural process—no one is exempt from it—but we should have the expectation to enjoy a healthy, strong, functioning, and beautiful body right up until we take our last breath. Jesus taught us to pray:

> *Your Kingdom come Your will be done, On earth as it is in heaven* (Matthew 6:10).

In Heaven there is no sickness, disease, weakness, or injury. There is nothing broken, nothing missing. If you have faith for this, step out and believe for these benefits to manifest in your life here on earth as it is in Heaven. Moses' sight did not grow dim and he did not lose his strength as he aged. Why not you too?

We will reap what we sow. If we sow health into our body, we will reap. There is no time like the present to start.

Look at the following attributes and see which one best describes you.

CATEGORY 1

Energized

Healthy

Great Immune System

Super Muscle Tone

Awesome Shape

Perfect Weight

Vibrant Skin Tone

Sparkling Eyes

CATEGORY 2

Lacking Energy

Weak

Always Fighting Sickness

Flabby Muscles

Unwanted Bulges

Overweight

Drab Skin Tone

Dull Eyes

If you discovered that Category 2 best described you, then you are among the majority of individuals in America in their mid-40s and over. If you would prefer to be in Category 1, you can be. It doesn't need to be difficult—it can be fun and easy!

Within less than half a year of adjusting into new exciting patterns of diet, exercise, and rest, you could be well on your way to being slim, trim, healthy, energized, and enjoying a new outlook on life. You will be a shiner, ready to run the race that is set before you! Remember, the rest of your life can be the best yet! You can make it so.

If you are going to be fit in mind, emotions, and spirit, you need a strong body to facilitate it. The body has five basic needs for optimum health, all of which are all easy to fulfill.

1. Hydration

Over 75 percent of your body weight is water. Simply by drinking enough water every day, you can improve your health and vitality. You will notice improvement in skin tone, eye brightness, muscle comfort, energy, and general well-being.

For optimum health, adequate water consumption is important. Most adults need about 64 ounces per day. That is 8 glasses of 8 ounces each. If you are working in warm weather, working out, on a weight-loss regime, detoxing, or fighting sickness, you will probably want to drink more. It is best to drink 50 percent of your water consumption between the time you wake up and lunch and the other half between lunch and the time you go to bed.

The following are some of the benefits of water on your body:

1. Transports nutrients throughout the body.
2. Rids the body of waste and flushes out toxins that are stored in muscles, tissues, and organs.
3. Helps to maintain proper blood volume in the body.
4. Aids in preventing constipation and helps the bowels function properly.
5. Keeps organs in the body supple.
6. Lubricates body organs (i.e., moistens eyes, mouth, nose).
7. Hydrates skin and helps it to maintain youthfulness.
8. Helps regulate body temperature, especially in warm weather.
9. Helps to suppress appetite.
10. Boosts metabolism (when drunk cold).
11. Helps to prevent urinary tract infections.
12. Helps organs to function well.
13. Forces fat to be used as fuel and helps avoid extra fat deposits.
14. Is a calorie-free beverage.
15. Helps the brain to function better and therefore potentially can sharpen your thinking.

Beverages such as coffee, sodas, and alcohol actually dehydrate you and should not be included in your total for water consumption. In fact, if you drink a cup of coffee, some say that you need to re-hydrate by drinking three volumes of water for every volume of coffee.

Drinking adequate water will refresh you, help you lose weight, and increase your overall health and vitality.

2. Nutrition

Your body needs good nutrition in order to serve you well. If you fill your body with all kinds of junk food and garbage then your body will respond accordingly. In Western culture, we are inundated with food that has been injected with chemicals and hormones that are not healthy for us. In the second half of life you want to put good, healthy, quality food into your system. Some say, "You are what you eat."

When you grocery shop make sure you fill your basket with whole grains, fresh fruit and vegetables, lean meat and poultry, and organic dairy products. These foods are usually found on the outside perimeters of the grocery store. I remember someone advising me to ONLY shop the outside aisles of the grocery store. If I did, they assured me that I would save money and eat healthier. They were right.

Vitamins, Minerals, and Natural Hormone Supplements

As you age, good vitamin, mineral, and natural hormone supplements are helpful to promote health and energy. Due to the massive amounts of processed and non-organic foods we eat, we lack nutrition. This can be made up with daily doses of good quality supplements. I would suggest making an appointment with a credible nutritionist or herbalist. Study out the various benefits of supplements and find out which ones are the best quality for your needs.

Green Stuff

I will never forget the day when Shirley Ross, the producer of our television show, presented me with this yucky drink that was apparently filled with vitamins and minerals. I had been suffering from a cold and she was convinced it would give me strength. She called it the "Green Stuff." It was filled with vitamins, antioxidants, and other really good energizing agents. It was 100 percent natural—and it actually worked. So, I frequently take it to this day. It still tastes terrible, but hey, it gives such a great boost. It has been beneficial for my general health and vitality.

There are many products available to aid in developing optimum health. I personally believe it is a good investment. With a very busy schedule, full of pressure, I need a healthy body in order to fulfill everything on my docket each day.

3. Exercise

In order to keep fit and energized in the second half of life, daily exercise is extremely important. It is good for your overall health and keeps the heart pumping well, muscles fit, and thinking clear.

If you are athletic, then it may not only be beneficial to your health but can also enhance your social life through joining a tennis or golf league or other team sports activity. I knew a man who began to snow ski in his 50s. He was amazing on the slopes. At the time of this writing, he is in his 80s and he looks fantastic. He is still full of energy, very fit, and enjoys vibrant health. Regular sports activities are enjoyable as well as physically beneficial. Just don't take on too much, too fast, and don't overdo it—ever!

There are all sorts of fitness clubs, exercise videos, and gym programs that are designed for those in the second half of life. My father-in-law daily engaged in water-aerobics when he retired. That little bit of daily exercise helped to keep him in good shape even into his 80's. His instructor taught the class until she was 93. Believe me, she didn't look or act her age. She got her students working hard each moment. I know, because I was a guest in the session a few times. She gave me a good workout!

If you are not accustomed to exercising then start out with a little each day—even 15 or 20 minutes is better than nothing. I would suggest having some good professional counsel on an exercise regime that would be suited for you. Start out slow and then build up.

My mother-in-law walked with a friend for one hour every night after dinner. It was a nice time to visit with her friend as well as get some exercise. You can take advantage of all kinds of activities throughout the day as well. For example, instead of driving to the post office or store, maybe walk the entire way or park the car a couple of blocks away and walk the rest. If you have stairs in your home, run up and down them a few times in a row each day. Vacuum through your entire house an extra time each week, and instead of using a sponge mop for the floor, try getting down on your hands and knees and giving them a good vigorous scrub with your arms. And of course, don't underestimate the clicking of the remote control on the television—great exercise for the fingers. My husband loves to push the mute button on and off in every commercial. You want to keep those fingers nimble! I am sure he does it for the exercise—smile. These are all little things that can help add a little extra to your exercise regime.

It seems that flat tummies are challenging to keep tight in both men and women in the second half of life. Usually this can be rectified easily by doing some simple tummy tightening exercises. Start with just a few of them when you wake up in the morning. Do a few more before going to bed at night. Even 15 or so to begin with is better than nothing. Every little effort will bring a measure of improvement. This goes for the saggy arm muscles and the drooping buttocks too. It can all be adjusted with some commitment. Don't think of it as a grueling task but as an absolute joyous opportunity.

Remember in an earlier chapter when we talked about attitude being everything? Well, you can apply this principle with exercise too. You can choose to enjoy exercise sessions. If you don't yet, simply change your attitude. Make a quality decision to *love* exercise. Come on now, say it... *"I love exercise."*

4. Detoxification

Detoxing is important for optimum health due to the amount of toxins that we ingest each day. Toxins are in the air we breathe and in just about everything we eat and drink. Stress also aids in the retention of toxins. Their presence in your system will cause your body to have to work harder to function. Many toxins fight against your immune system and fill your blood, muscles, brain cells, nerves, elimination system, and body organs with poisons that rob you of strength, health, and general well-being. Toxins can affect your emotional well-being and mental alertness as well as your physical health. You do not want toxins in your system at all, but in the world we live in, it is difficult to eliminate them completely. A strong immune system, however, will overpower their effects and diminish their influence. Detoxing cleanses your body from toxins and gives the immune system time to be fortified. Detox programs should not only involve the elimination of toxins but should also include nutritional supplements that build up your immune system and general health at the same time.

There are many nutritional supplements, cleansers, teas, and juices, easily obtained in most health centers, that help with the process of eliminating toxins and purifying your body. There are herbal blood cleansers, colon cleansers, cleansers that help to eliminate metals from your system, and those that cleanse the liver and kidneys from toxins.

Most detoxing involves fasting from the very foods that carry the toxins. The detoxing usually takes a number of weeks, even up to 40 days, but most individuals feel great after engaging in these regimes. Before detoxing it is very important that you study out your options and confer with a trusted professional nutritionist.

The first time I detoxed was remarkable. I had been tired, experienced loss of energy, and had frequent back and headaches. My skin and eyes looked dull and my hair lacked shine. I went on a high quality, three-week colon cleanser that included great nutritional supplements. I drank around 10 glasses of purified water each day and only ate pure foods (fresh organic fruit and vegetables, herbal teas, whole grains without yeast, and fresh juice).

During the first week of the three-week regime, I felt very sick. I suffered migraines, increased aches in my muscles and lower back, skin eruptions, bad breath, and terrible body odor. Believe it or not, these are all signs of successful detoxing. The toxins were being eliminated and were finding their way out of the body. I have to admit that after three days I wanted to abort the process, but I was encouraged to carry on. After the fourth day, the symptoms lessened, and by the eighth day I was actually feeling great. Each day after that, I noticed remarkable improvement. It was almost unbelievable. By the end of the three weeks, my face shone, my eyes sparkled and my long, blond hair (at the time) had a beautiful natural sheen. I experienced crystal clear thinking and mental alertness, my energy level was over-the-top, my spiritual alertness was at high levels, and I felt like a million bucks! That first experience has sold me on the benefits of detoxing. As a matter of fact, as I am writing this, I am getting so charged that I want to start another one right now!

It has been suggested to me that detoxing twice a year for 20-40 days will keep your body cleansed.

Massage

Professional massage is beneficial to the detoxing regime. Muscles house toxins. When the muscles are properly massaged, the stress in the muscles is eliminated. The toxins are dislodged, move into the lymph nodes, and then are eliminated. Following massage, it is important to drink lots of water to help with the detoxing process.

5. Rest

In order for your body to function well, it must rejuvenate. Sleep and rest allow your body's organs and cells to rejuvenate and get refreshed. As you age, you may find that your sleep is interrupted. In menopause, women often have hot and cold spells at night that interrupt sleep. It is a fact that the natural sleep hormone, melatonin, depletes as we age. I personally take a health supplement of melatonin each night and it aids my sleep (stay away from sleeping pills if at all possible—they are habit-forming and are not healthy to consume). There are also many herbs and vitamins available to help with the menopausal symptoms.

A wellness coach once informed me that the body requires at least four hours of continuous, uninterrupted sleep in order to rejuvenate. Whenever possible attempt to secure that four hours in one sleep session. If you have trouble sleeping, however, the worst thing to do is to worry. Just relax. Lie and rest. Pray. Meditate and think on those things that are good and pleasant. Soak in some good worship music on your iPod and allow your spirit man to get strengthened. Ask the Lord to supernaturally rejuvenate you. He can and He will.

The Everlasting God, the Lord, The Creator of the ends of the earth Does not become weary or tired His understanding is inscrutable. He gives strength to the weary, And to him who lacks might He increases power.... Yet those who wait for the Lord Will gain new strength; They will mount up with wings like eagles, They will run and not get tired, They will walk and not become weary (Isaiah 40:28-29,31).

At 53 years of age, I noticed a remarkable change in my sleep patterns. I had never experienced interrupted sleep until then. At first I worried, but soon found that stressing out over it was no solution. Now if I happen to wake up and can't get back to sleep, I lie and pray or worship. Sometimes I get up and read my Bible or work for a few hours and then go back to sleep later. Because I make the sleep interruption work in my favor I find that I am seldom tired the next day as a result.

Power Naps

Power naps can be extremely helpful. I am one of those people who can lay my head on a pillow, drop off into a deep sleep immediately, and then wake up 15-20 minutes later feeling as perky as can be. If you are like this, then take advantage of the blessing. Those little power naps will refresh you for the hours to come.

Many, however, do not have that ability programmed into their system. It is still beneficial to take a "power rest." Just lie down for 15-20 minutes in the midst of your day or early evening and meditate on peaceful things. Soak. Relax. These little "power rests" also bring refreshment.

Weight Loss

Now, this subject is a "biggie." Weight gains and slower metabolism seem to be a common complaint amongst the over-40 crowd.

The thing with weight gain is that in most cases it carries a big lie. It works like this: you look at yourself in the mirror and you think, "Oh my gosh, look at how ugly I am with this extra fat. My clothes are tight, flab is hanging over my belt, my eyes are puffy, and my cheeks look swollen." So usually you try to do something about it, like charge into a lose-weight-quick diet and massive exercise regime. It works for a little while and then your insatiable appetite returns along with the full-on craving for chocolate-chip cookies and Twinkies. You miss a few exercise classes. Then you are too busy to return. The fat comes back along with a few added pounds. You brave it and in another month or so, you go through the whole regime again. Does this sound familiar?

After a few cycles of this pattern, you lose hope. Your mind tells you, "You can't do anything about this. This problem is bigger than you are. You have tried and failed. You are fat and ugly and that is it. Live with it."

The failures have produced pain until the lie becomes established. If you live out of the lie, you will let yourself go, not even attempting to look your best. You will buy bigger and bigger sizes and lose that healthy pride in your appearance. You will end up taking on the "fat and frumpy" image, trying to make yourself believe that it is okay—after all, it is the inner person that counts. The problem is, in these cases, the inner person actually believes they are fat, ugly, and defeated. It is all one big lie! Don't fall into it! Just keep fighting; you will win. That's right. You can and you will. Your victory is just around the corner. Don't give in to defeat!

Let me share with you my personal testimony and journey in this area.

My Story

When I was younger I had lots of energy, rarely got sick, had great muscle tone without focusing on exercise, and was able to eat massive amounts of food and not struggle with weight gain. I noticed a change in my body around the time I turned 45. I noticed things like flabby muscles, hair where I didn't want it, and gradual weight gain—about 10 pounds per year. That is actually less than 1 pound per month but after four years I packed on 40 pounds and had gone from a size 14 to a size 20. In the last year of the weight gain, I could feel the skin on my thighs rubbing together when I walked, I huffed and puffed going up stairs, and I was generally feeling weak and tired most of the time, yet I needed to keep a very busy schedule. I was constantly fighting colds, chest conditions, Candida yeast infections, and muscle aches. I was diagnosed with bronchial asthma as a result of a compromised immune system. I was discouraged, to say the least. I had lost some of my joy and zest for life. What a horrible way to live.

I kept thinking, "I really need to do something about my health and get this excessive weight off." As long as you say, "I really need to," you won't. Somewhere along the line, you have to bite the bullet and say, "I'm going to," then immediately plunge into the battle!

During a speaking engagement in New Jersey, I had some God-appointed help to assist me in making the decision. I had ministered in that church the year before. The pastor's wife, who was a fairly large woman, sat me down one morning and said, "I'm not really qualified to talk to you about this because I myself am greatly overweight, but I have noticed that you have gained weight this year. If I were you I would do something about it!" Yikes, those words penetrated deep! This was my fourth year in gaining weight, and yes, I did need to break the pattern—but how?

It was discouraging to hear that my weight gain was so noticeable, as I thought I was hiding it well by wearing bigger, looser clothing. I was, however, grateful for the confrontation. I love to eat and I don't like feeling restricted. I like flexibility and have never liked the idea of dieting. How could I do this and still be happy? I was only in my mid-40s. I had a whole life to live. Was it going to be miserable? Restricting?

I went to prayer and poured my heart out to God. I knew I would need His wisdom and strength. I determined after prayer that evening to make a quality decision to do something about it—now!

I thought, "Well, it took me four years to get this weight on, so even if it takes me a year or two to get it off it is better than gaining another 10 pounds by this time next year."

Some of you might be thinking, "But I have so much to lose—it will take forever to get it all off!" I know the feeling. It is comforting to know though that you can draw the line in the sand and say, "This year, I am not gaining one more pound—this is it!" If your goal is to successfully maintain your weight, then if you lose 10 pounds a year, it is a real bonus…and that, dear friend, is less than a pound a month to lose. And the other important factor is, if you lose weight sensibly through simple adjustments in diet and exercise, then you will increase your energy, stamina, and health. My turnaround came from being willing to make a long-term commitment.

The first thing I did was to establish a 30-minute brisk walk into my daily routine. I had not done any physical exercise for years and it showed. I didn't change my diet at first, because I didn't want to start one and stay on it for short term. I wanted something that would work for me forever so I needed to investigate my options first.

The walking helped tremendously. I kept thinking, *This is more than what I did before. Instead of getting worse, I am getting better, even if it is in baby steps.* At first the half hour walk seemed to be an eternity, and I must say that it took discipline to get out that door and do it. But once I was on my way, it was great—it was just making that initial decision that was the greatest hurdle. I learned to say, "I am going for my walk now," rather than, "I should go on a walk," or "I need to go on a walk." If you hear yourself saying, "I need to" or "I should" then you won't. Change your decree to "I will" or "I am going to…now." After a number of days, the 30-minute walk was easy and went by quickly. Before I knew it, I was enjoying 45-minute walks and sometimes even 60- and 90-minute power strolls. I used the time to meditate and pray and ponder the day ahead of me. My body started feeling a measure of refreshment and vitality within the first week.

A friend of mine, who had been through fitness training, explained to me that if I never changed my diet, but committed to walking a brisk 30-minute walk a day I could lose 10 pounds of weight a year, tone up the body, and feel better overall. That inspired me to go for it and develop the discipline as part of my lifestyle. I continued to walk my daily walks for four years. I then got busy and let it slip a little here and a little there until I completely backslid…and my body showed it. I once again started to feel tired, stressed, gained some weight back, and was discouraged.

Don't ever whine over things—it doesn't help at all. I've tried every type of whining over the years and they have all failed, so don't even go there. Simply make a quality decision to get back on track. Once you make the initial quality decision to get out the door for the walk, usually within 5 minutes you are glad you did. The things that you would have chosen to do instead can almost always wait. Speak to your unruly flesh and say, "*You* are going for a walk—now!"

I realize that some of you may not be able to walk, so your form of exercise may be different. Whatever your choice of exercise is, commit to it and stay focused. If you lose some ground through "backsliding," renew your quality decision and command your flesh to get into line. You are the boss over it! If you make an investment into your health every day, you will reap the benefits for years to come. No matter how many times you fail in trying to get back, just keep renewing your commitment to go for it. One of those times you will make it over the hurdle. When you do, keep running and don't look back!

The daily walking really helped, but I also needed to do something about my diet. I had packed on so much weight that I was uncomfortable with it. Friends were making discreet suggestions about how I should try this and that to get some weight off. How embarrassing! I couldn't hide my dilemma. Everybody noticed.

As an itinerant speaker, I am always being treated to meals out, luscious deserts, snacks after meetings, and all kinds of treats in speaker's baskets that are prepared by the host groups. Yes, cookies, chips, nuts, chocolate bars, and sodas await me in those speaker's baskets. They sit and stare at you every night on the dressers in hotel rooms. Those baskets are so beautiful—pretty wrappings, bows.... Back in my struggle days, they contained an irresistible temptation to charge deep into their midst to discover the contents...then eat them of course. For years I spoke at up to three venues per week, so that is a lot of baskets!

I looked at different options: calorie counting, low fat diets, weight-loss clinic diets, and all kinds of other weight-loss diets and regimes. All of them seemed like so much work and so restrictive. I wanted a diet that was good for my health, simple, uncomplicated for me to follow, and something that gave me freedom and enjoyment.

Everyone's needs are different, but let me share with you what worked for me. A friend shared with me that she had gone on the Atkins diet. This diet is low carbohydrate and high protein. She looked fabulous and had lost a ton of weight. As a result, I bought the book and read through it thoroughly. After reading through the material, I was convinced that this was the diet for me. I love meat, cheese, sour cream, cream, butter, and all those types of food. I found out that with this particular diet I could eat what I loved without restriction on the amounts, lose weight, and walk in great health (yes, that's right—don't judge if you haven't read all the material by its founders). With this diet, I understood that I would need to follow it carefully or it could work against my health and weight-loss goals rather than fulfill them. There could be *no* cheating! I put the book down and committed to it immediately. I had both the desire and the faith for it. I could hardly wait.

For breakfast I would have bacon and eggs with tomato slices or a vegetable omelet with cottage cheese. For lunch I would have a tuna salad, a Greek salad, or delicious low-carb soup. For dinner I ate vegetables like fresh broccoli, cauliflower, asparagus, and green beans, as well as salad, and generous portions of meat, poultry, or fish. For desert I would have sugar-free JellO or a small dish of strawberries or blueberries with fresh whipping cream. For grains I would eat a puffed-rice cake and sometimes put cheese, tuna, chicken, or egg salad on it. I drank 8-12 glasses of water a day. When I was hungry I would have a piece of cheese or a stalk of celery with some cream cheese. I went for it wholeheartedly—and loved it.

Before I started this diet my belly was all bloated, my face was puffy, and I was very lethargic. I discovered that many people who eat large amounts of carbohydrate and sugar in their diet struggle with these symptoms. One of the main reasons is related to our insulin balance. Known as the "fat-storing hormone," *insulin* is the hormone that determines if food will be burned off or stored as fat. When you eat carbs and sugars, your blood sugar is elevated and insulin is released to bring balance. If you do not need the energy then your cells will store it. Carbs and sugars elevate the blood sugar quickly—they are quick energy foods. The problem is, when you eat too many of them too often, your cells become filled with excess energy due to storage of unused calories, then you gain weight. When released, the insulin knows your body does not need the energy and so stores it as fat in the cells.

Most of us, as we get older, experience some changes in our metabolism due to insulin resistance. This explains why many of us gain weight as we age. As we get older, we do not require as many carbs and sugars for energy as we did when we were younger.

A sign of what I would call carb-sugar toxicity is the evidence of thickness around the middle in both men and women. For men, they sometimes call it a "beer belly." That is because beer is loaded with carbs and sugar and, when people overindulge, it produces a storage of unused energy in the belly. Women often get thick around the reproductive area as a result of raised insulin levels, while their cells are filled with all the energy they need. The consumption of any amount of sugar or carbs at that point will be converted into fat and stored in the cells, making the thickness around the middle thicker. Excessive carb and sugar intake is usually the culprit for the thick belly syndrome, especially in a culture where we eat so much junk food that is full of carbs and sugars as well as the unhealthy type of fat (trans-fat).

While carbs and sugar release insulin quickly, fat and protein consumption releases insulin more slowly. The Atkins diet and other low carbohydrate diets such as Suzanne Somers' have discovered that the right kind of fat actually burns fat rather than stores it.

It all sounded good to me, so I went for it. I wanted a strong, healthy body full of energy and vitality. I made a quality commitment to change my eating patterns. For me, this was not to be a quick-fix diet but a change in lifestyle. I wanted the extra weight off but I wasn't in a hurry. It had taken me four years to pack it on, so even if it took me four years to get it back off, I was committed. No quick fixes.

It is a good thing I had that attitude because for the first three weeks I felt rather weak and sometimes queasy in my stomach. I realized that I was in carb and sugar withdrawal. I was toxic and needed to get the poisons out of my system. Another interesting thing was that in the first three weeks I never lost one pound. I was eating healthier though. No junk food. No sugar. Lots of water, vegetables, proteins, and fat-burning fats.

After the third week, all the symptoms of feeling toxic left and I lost almost 10 pounds in one week. That was a major encouragement. I hit a plateau for another month and then dropped some more. In less than four months I had lost almost the full 40 pounds I had put on. I felt great. I had energy to spare. I didn't have any dips in my energy level and I felt clear in my thinking. I loved it. For me, this eating pattern worked.

Everyone has to discover their own preference, and I am in no way suggesting that this diet is for you, but it was and is amazing for me. I found it easy to stick to in restaurants and while on the road. I simply stood my ground and said, "I don't do carbs or sugars." It was easy and enjoyable.

I stayed on that eating pattern for over three years without compromising. On the maintenance part of this plan you can have about 40 grams of carbs a day which gave me what I needed. I continued to feel good, maintained my weight and energy, and was not sick during that time. All the Candida, asthma, colds, etc., cleared up. I was told that the reason why I did not get sick or struggle with infections was due to the Atkins diet producing an alkaline balance in my body. Some medical nutritionists agree that in an alkaline system, disease finds it hard to live. They further believe that disease actually develops and flourishes in an acid environment. The acid environment can be produced in our bodies when we eat carbs and sugars.

Many of my friends were freaked out with me being on Atkins. They had read books that were anti-Atkins and thought I was going to suffer a heart attack or something. I did allow some of the negativity to get to me. After three successful years, I decided to take a year and eat more fruit and grains as they suggested. The first year went fine, but my appetite for carbs and sugars began to grow…and grow…and grow. After the first year, I found myself binging on carbs and sugars until the same symptoms I had previously returned.

My weight started to come back slowly. I was developing cravings again for sugar that were hard to break. Once again I suffered from a compromised immune system and began getting hit with colds, chest infections, and general malaise at times. I had no need to divert from my low-carb lifestyle. I shouldn't have. For me, it was the best.

During a year of high stress in 2006 and 2007, I also discovered myself falling into the lie of comforting myself with food. I felt pain within and wanted to be comforted. When I ate something sweet, it made me momentarily feel good inside. The problem is, the type of comfort derived from food is very short lived, but the excess fat gets stored in the system for the long term—that "comfort" equaled about 25 pounds of weight gain. You will be able to handle emotional stress and pain much easier if you are physically refreshed and well nourished. The Holy Spirit is the true Comforter. You can be filled with as much of Him as you want without gaining a single pound.

I am finally back on track and doing well. Things are settling once again and my health is returning.

You may be led differently as it is important that you find the right eating pattern for you. But let me give you some pointers that I learned to help you with diet and weight loss:

1. Make a quality decision to move toward your goal. Put things in motion.

2. Never skip a meal. If you do, your body will go into fasting mode and will hold on to the calories that you consume later. It will be stored as fat. Skipping meals is a sure way to slow down your metabolism. You should never go more than three hours without eating something.

3. Eliminate junk food from your diet—that includes diet sodas, diet foods, chips, fast foods, and sugars. America's junk food is poison to your system. Put good, wholesome food into your body. If you are not ready to eliminate all junk foods, then start by diminishing the amounts that you consume. For

example, let's say you drink four cans of diet soda per day; even if you reduce that by one it is better than no change at all (remember that diet sodas have been known to be more damaging to your health than the sugar-filled sodas).

4. Look for snacks that will fill your body with nutrition. Be creative and have them available for when you crave something.

5. Eat natural food as much as possible. Butter, for example, is better for you than margarine.

6. Choose a diet that has food options that you love and be creative in your meal planning.

7. Drink lots of water.

8. Add an extra 30 minutes of exercise per day to your schedule. If you are not ready to commit to 30 minutes then try even five minutes at first. Anything is better than nothing. If you are used to doing 30 minutes per day, then go for 35 or 45. Increase it just a little and you will see results.

9. If you slip, then get right back on track. Don't binge and say, "I might as well really go for it now and start afresh tomorrow." No, get back on track right away.

10. Eat until you're satisfied. Don't overeat.

11. Have a goal for the long term. Make this a lifestyle change rather than "going on a diet."

12. Be patient—don't worry about how fast the weight comes off. Draw a line in the sand and say, "As of today, I am not increasing in weight, ever again." It

took you probably a good many months or years to put the weight on, so be patient in how fast it comes off.

Appearance

It is always important to look your best, especially when you feel your worst. If you are overweight, then spiff yourself up and look the very best you can. Take pride in your appearance.

At my 20-year high school reunion, I noticed that the women (all of them close to 40) were babes. They looked fantastic! They had taken care of their figures, wore trendy clothes, and generally looked really cool! The majority of the men, on the other hand, had let themselves go. Most of them were overweight, had beer-bellies, and looked a bit scruffy.

About seven years later, I met a couple of my classmates while traveling. In seven years they had aged and took on the frumpy mode. So had I. It jolted me. We seemed to have lost respect for our outer appearance as we grew older.

My life is all about God. I am a God-fanatic and yes, you could call me a Jesus-freak! I am totally consumed by Him. I think of Him all day long. He is the Number One Love of my life. I am "crazy-in-love" with Him!

One of the things I have come to know about God is that He is majorly into appearance. He created and fashioned humankind in His image, and the Bible teaches us that He is altogether glorious and full of splendor. That means we are too. He clothed Adam in so much glory that Adam didn't see his nakedness until after he sinned. There is no ugliness in Heaven or in God—He is altogether lovely. His Word tells us that we are "fearfully [awesomely] and wonderfully made" (Ps. 139:14). Each of us is absolutely stunning in His sight!

God is also interested in clothing design. He is the most amazing designer in the universe. Throughout the Bible, you will see the care and attention He gives to details, especially when He designed the priestly garments and instructed Moses on how they should be made, complete with gems (see Exod. 28). In the New Testament, Jesus teaches that God is the One who clothes the lilies of the field (see Matt. 6:27-29).

Everything in Heaven is beautiful, dazzling, and full of splendor. When Jesus was transfigured, Matthew 17:2 describes Him in the following manner: "...His face shone like the sun, and His garments became as white as light." Moses and Elijah were also there in the midst of this heavenly glory. Jesus was amazingly stunning! And, so are you! You were created as an object of beauty. As you believe this you will manifest this beauty.

Don't let the world dictate to you how you are to dress or look, yet at the same time, you don't need to make a statement against the world by not caring for your appearance. I truly believe that those of us in our second half of life can look absolutely drop-dead gorgeous...so much so that people will stop and take notice. We don't desire to draw attention to ourselves, of course, but we do want to shine as lights...and people can see light!

Abraham had a wife named Sarah. In her 80s she was so stunning in her outer beauty that Pharaoh, who thought she was Abraham's sister, actually wanted to take her for his wife. Wow. That Sarah syndrome is really something. That is a lot of beauty!

I believe that inner beauty is way more important than outer beauty. Sarah was known for the inner beauty of her heart (see 1 Pet. 3) and yet it obviously affected her outer appearance. She was a wowzer, inside and out. You can be too. Make a quality decision to look your best ever in the second half of life.

Years ago, I knew a woman who was so lovely and yet outwardly was dowdy in her appearance. I asked her if I could treat her to a makeover. She agreed. I treated her to a make-up session, hair cut, and a new outfit. Oh my gosh! She was stunning—and she loved it. Everyone noticed and made comments on how beautiful she looked. That was a turning point for her. She carried on with enhancing her beauty.

I have noticed that sometimes after women get married that they lose the motivation to make themselves look their best. Perhaps in the busyness of life, looking after chores, children, and employment outside the home, it gets difficult to focus. I do think it is important, though. It is also important for men to care for themselves. I know of women who have lost interest in their husbands because they no longer cared about their appearance or hygiene. I have also noticed men do the same—they let themselves go. We should always look our best, no matter how old we are.

Brain Fitness

It is important to exercise your brain functions and reasoning capacities as you age. You don't want to grow dull of mind. Keep mentally alert and sharp. My father-in-law did crossword puzzles every day to keep his mind alert. There are many such thought-provoking games available today. Some card and board games like chess or bridge are good to grow in mental precision and focus.

My grandfather took two college courses each year after age 65 at an adult education center. He had a blast! He was always the oldest in his classes but he loved being around the younger crowd. They kept him youthful in his outlook and his mind sharpened as a result of the learning process.

Read lots of books and do some mathematical exercises. Both those activities exercise a different part of the brain. Choose activities that stimulate your mental alertness. Be careful not to spend too much time in front of a television. Learning a new craft or skill is helpful for mental alertness, too, and helps you to express your creativity. These things can be fun. You can learn to do things you have never done before. It is never too late to learn something new.

The Beautiful You!

You were created to manifest beauty inside and out. You are an amazing individual who has more to give in the second half of life than the first. You need your health, strength, and vitality as many new adventures await you. Do whatever it takes—and enjoy it.

CHAPTER EIGHT

Step Into Greater Glory

(A Prophetic Conclusion)

I am absolutely convinced that the generation who is in their second half of life is now going to arise and shine. What do they look like? They are a people full of love, wisdom, humility, grace, miracle-working power, and glory. They are a fearless generation who are loaded with courage and tenacity.

They are a generation who have gleaned understanding from the hard lessons in life and have persevered with endurance and faith. They are absolutely breathtaking in appearance as the purity of their hearts reflects great glory and light through the outer shell of their body.

They are a generation who are full of vitality and who will run alongside of the next generation with a generous heart of support and love. They restore righteous foundations and do not fear to speak when called to uphold godly morals and principles. They are a selfless generation who care about others more than themselves.

They are a generation who live in fullness and enjoy all the blessings offered by God. Filled with joy, they brighten the world around them giving hope to the hopeless. This generation will never be forgotten in the history of man.

This generation is you!

Go in peace!

Run your race in fullness—all the way to the end.

The latter glory of the house is greater than the former.

The best is yet to come.

God Loves You With an Everlasting Love (Booklet)

God Loves You with an Everlasting Love *booklet by Patricia King— permission granted to print. Copyright 2003, Patricia King.*

A NOTE FROM THE DESK OF PATRICIA KING:

Dear Reader,

There is nothing better in life than knowing beyond any doubt that you are unconditionally and perfectly loved! Countless individuals spend their entire lives attempting to satisfy the cries of the empty and lonely places within—the places that long for the comfort and security that only love can provide.

Where is such love and satisfaction found? Can you really experience that kind of security and well-being? Is it actually possible to understand the value of who you were created to be?

This booklet is designed to introduce you to the greatest revelation anyone could ever receive. It is the revelation of God's unconditional love for you—the love that was perfectly tested and proven at the cross, 2,000 years ago.

There is no one like you. You were created as an object of His affection, acceptance, and love. It was never God's desire for you to experience rejection or abandonment; you were made to be a recipient of His bountiful grace and favor.

May you drink deeply of this revelation and come to a full realization that:

God loves you with an everlasting love!

Patricia King

The God Kind of Love

"Behold, what manner of love the Father hath bestowed upon us, *that we should be called the sons of God…*" (1 John 3:1 KJV, emphasis mine).

What manner of love would motivate a perfect, holy, and righteous God to offer a sinful and rebellious person the opportunity to become His very own dear child and heir of all that He is and all that He has? It sounds extravagant, doesn't it? This, however, is indeed the very manner of love the Father has shown to each and every one of us. Nothing throughout the history of mankind has ever been able to make Him withdraw this love, although we have all put His love to the test, over and over again. The demonstration of this love is unchangeable because He is unchangeable.

Many individuals regularly waver in their feelings of assurance of God's love and continually question their right standing with Him. This lack of assurance breeds insecurity. They might ask, "Am I worthy enough? Do I love God enough? Am I performing well enough? Am I serving Him enough?"

My own faith constantly wavered before I understood the clear revelation of Christ's work on the cross that demonstrated His eternal, unchangeable love for me. During those years, I always questioned my value in His sight. This produced striving, tension, and unrest. Without the assurance of His unchanging love one is never free to be. If not free to be, one will never be free to do. It is the revelation of His love that produces fullness, freedom, and fruitfulness in life.

First John 4:18-19 (NKJV) teaches us that, "We love Him because He first loved us" and "There is no fear in love." When you understand the unconditional love of God, the fear of not being accepted and loved by Him is eliminated. You know deep within you're His precious one, and you're assured of your place in His heart forever. When you have that assurance, you feel secure, even when everything in life is unsettled. Love gives you an unshakable confidence that He will work everything out and keep you in perfect peace.

Romans 8:32-39 informs us that the love the Father has given us is greater than any other force. It confidently assures us that nothing can separate us from His love. In fact, you can never be separated from the love of God that is in Christ Jesus—**never.** In Christ, you are forever sealed in His holy love. Oh, how wonderful!

You (like most everyone else) probably weren't loved unconditionally in your childhood, so from time to time lying thoughts may have assaulted your mind. *I'm not lovable. I'm not accepted. I haven't been able to accomplish enough. I have no value. I can't succeed.*

The Word, however, says that you are perfectly loved and that nothing at all can ever separate you from the source of that love. When you really start to understand this truth, you will be able to cast down the tormenting lies of rejection, inferiority, and insecurity. The power of God's love and favor will prevail, causing the lies to fall. Then you will experience what you were created to be from the foundation of the world—an object of His deep love and affection.

God wants you to feel so secure in His love that you will be able to go anywhere, do anything, face any spirit of rejection, and overcome any obstacle. You will able to say with confidence, "I am a precious, loved child of God. I am His favored one."

Love is God's mark on our lives. Not only are we to know His love for ourselves, but we are to extravagantly share it with others. Once you know you are a loved one, His love in you will spill out all over the place and touch others—you won't be able to help it! This type of love doesn't come from an inward striving to be a loving person. It comes from knowing who you are as a perfectly loved child. Then His powerful grace flows through you like a river and offers refreshing to those around you.

A Personal Testimony

I remember clearly what life was like without Christ and the revelation of His love. I was a young career woman, a wife, and the mother of two boys, yet totally unfulfilled and broken. Most of my brokenness, however, was hidden to the onlooker. I wore an invisible mask of well-being because I was afraid to let people see the real me. What if they rejected me? How could I ever cope with that? I lived behind the many disguises that concealed the guilt and shame plaguing my heart. I was in an invisible prison, and I couldn't escape.

I tried everything to become free. I attended numerous self-help courses and joined New Age/occult enlightenment groups, hoping to find some answers for my distressed soul. I regularly imbibed in a variety of addictive substances in an effort to find comfort and relief. I also attempted to find meaning for life through my career and taking extra college courses. Every effort failed to offer any liberty. I became increasingly unstable emotionally, with no way to get a grip on things. The more I tried, the more I failed. The more I failed, the more discouraged and bound I became. The tentacles of fear, shame, and guilt wrapped themselves around me, strangling any tinge of hope. I was constantly plagued with a sense of powerlessness in life. I was a mess, totally out of control! I desperately needed help but didn't know where to turn.

God hears the cries of our heart, and He definitely heard mine. It was following a near-death experience, at the lowest point of my life, that the Lord sent a wonderful man to share the gospel with me. He was an Anglican minister named Reverend Ron Hunt. I will never forget the first evening I attended a little home Bible study at his invitation. Although I was nervous to step into that unfamiliar environment, I was pleasantly surprised as I witnessed a sincere group of people who obviously knew God in a very personal way. One after another that evening, they shared testimonies of how Jesus had changed their lives. They claimed that He forgave their sins, cleansed them from guilt and shame, and offered them a brand new life. Wow! That was exactly what I wanted—but was it possible?

Returning home, I knelt on my living room floor and cried out to this unseen God for help. "Jesus, I have nothing to offer You except my brokenness. I have made a big mess of my life, but I would really like You to come into my heart and make me new, just like You did for those people up the street." I felt so evil, I didn't know if Jesus would want to come into my life or not. I had no confidence that He would be able to love the likes of me.

To my amazement, He didn't hesitate to enter my heart. I hadn't even finished praying when I literally felt the presence of liquid love come into my being. The One who knew every wicked detail of my life didn't hesitate, even for a moment, to show me His extravagant mercy and acceptance. I literally felt the pressure of my sin leave me along with all the guilt and shame. It was as though a prison door had been opened and I was allowed to run free. I felt lovely and beautiful inside for the very first time.

All I could do was cry. In fact, I cried all night while I worshiped Him. No one had to teach me to worship; when you are deeply touched by His love, worship is a normal response—the only response! Everything in you is thankful, so very grateful. I knew beyond a shadow of a doubt that this gift of love had nothing to do with my own ability to fix myself. My endless failed attempts had proven that I was "unfixable." This was a free gift of life—His gift of everlasting, unbendable, unchangeable, unshakable, and unfailing love! Yeah, God!

The next number of years were deeply fulfilling for me as I daily experienced increased revelation of His Word and ways. His love healed, delivered, and established me in a brand new life. It had nothing at all do with my efforts. This new life is His gift. It is a gift that can't be earned, and it is available to everyone. It is available to you!

I began to serve the Lord with passion. I never for a moment felt pressured to serve Him—I served Him because I loved Him. It's what you do when you're in love. My entire life changed. I had new friends, new interests, and new desires. I wanted to spend my entire life serving the One who had loved me so perfectly. One year after my rebirth, my husband began following Jesus. Year after year was filled with a continual unfolding of His goodness.

As a young Christian, I never tasted "legalism," the attempt to secure right standing with the Lord through obedience to the Law. I was first introduced to this type of religious bondage when our family served the Lord on a foreign mission field. The leaders of the mission center were very passionate for the Lord. And I know they meant well. Unfortunately, they did not understand that the Lord's unconditional love is a gift and cannot be earned through our works. As a result, they taught those they worked with to perfect themselves through self-effort in order to please God. The leaders themselves lived under this burden.

I experienced performance pressure daily on this mission field. In all my striving to do well, l believed I was constantly falling short of what was expected. I was convinced I was disappointing God, and the more I tried to please Him, the more I failed. The more I failed, the more I strove within. The cycle continued with increasing despair and pressure, taking me right back into the torment and bondage I had experienced prior to knowing Christ. I was plagued with the same guilt and the same shame, simply wearing different clothes. One was a cloak of unrighteousness, and the other was one of self-righteousness. Both bore the same fruit of devastation and were deadly.

After six months of serving on that mission field as faithfully and diligently as I could, I finished our term feeling spiritually bankrupt. I had even lost assurance of my salvation. I believed I had totally failed the Lord and that He would never have any use for me again. I believed that I was no longer a precious child to Him—I had disappointed Him too deeply. What a deception I had stepped into!

On our return home, friends helped me to rightly divide the Word and to trust that the Lord still loved me. The healing and restoration did not come overnight. At times I was still plagued with the fear of being rejected by God. I constantly battled self-condemnation and cried out for relief. All I wanted was to feel close to God—to feel worthy of His love and to know I was pleasing Him.

It was years later that I received a revelation of the cross. This revelation delivered me from the torment and fear that had bound my soul, and became an anchor for my faith forever. The revelation of the cross and the covenant Christ made with God on our behalf is the foundation for understanding His unconditional love. The day I received this revelation, I wept for hours on end, completely in awe of His loving-kindness, completely amazed at His grace.

It is one thing to be touched by the love of God and enjoy the experience of it, like I did as a young Christian. It is another thing, however, to be fully anchored in the unshakable, unfailing revelation of the doctrine of His unconditional love. Jesus said, "You shall know the truth, and the truth shall make you free" (John 8:32 NKJV). The day the revelation of the doctrine of the cross filled my heart was the day I knew I would walk free forever. Regardless of circumstances surrounding my life, regardless of condemning thoughts assaulting my mind, I now have an eternal place to stand. I was anchored forever in His love when I understood the truth of it! I am blood-bought into an eternal love covenant that can never be broken. What freedom this truth brings!

This booklet will introduce you to this life-changing, life-sustaining doctrine. May you come to know the revelation of this truth so deeply within your heart that your entire being will forever be filled and anchored in it. Walk through the following pages with expectation and focus as the Holy Spirit unfolds the most profound and life-altering doctrine in the entire Bible—the cross and the covenant. This doctrine reveals God's true heart of unfailing love. He loves you with an everlasting love—He really does. You will see!

God Chose You!

God wanted you! You weren't a mistake, regardless of the circumstances that surrounded your birth. Perhaps you weren't planned by your parents or your conception was the result of an unfortunate incident. You need to know that, even in cases as sad as these, God had you in His heart from before the foundation of the world. He planned you. His ultimate desire was for you to be conceived and brought forth in a beautiful, pure atmosphere of parental love and affection. Tragically, everyone has fallen short of His perfect ways because of our sinful, imperfect nature. God planned for you to come forth into the realm of time and fulfill His eternal purpose for your life. Exploring His potential in you is fun!

God actually wanted to have a family. That's why most folks desire to have children; that desire comes from Him. Humankind has been created in His likeness, and therefore, when you find yourself longing to have children, you are simply identifying with His passion. He wanted children, and that's why you do, too (unless you've been emotionally wounded or have a special call to remain single).

In the beginning, God created trees, flowers, birds, fish, animals, and a host of other earthly and celestial things. He loved everything He created, and each day He saw that "it was good" (Gen. 1:1-25 KJV). Even though He was very pleased, He still longed for a precious creation made in His likeness—an object of His affection to fulfill the longing of His righteous heart.

My husband Ron and I did not have children in our first year of marriage. We did, however, have two dogs. Although we enjoyed our dogs and they were like family, they did not satisfy our longing for children. The dogs were nice, but not *that* nice. There was something inside us that said, "Children, children, children." That longing was a small taste of what the Lord felt in His heart for us. Dogs, and other creatures, were not enough for Him, either. Although He took pleasure in them, they did not satisfy His desire to have **you**! Passionate desire for you was burning inside His heart. Envisioning you, He said, "I long for you; I desire to pour out My deep love, kindness, and goodness upon you."

God deeply desired children; yet, before man was ever created, God knew we were going to blow it. He wasn't caught off guard—He is the all-knowing One. As a result, before He even created us He initiated a plan to rescue our lives from the power of sin. The Bible calls this act "redemption." He actually took care for the problem for us before we had even acted out the problem. "The Lamb [was] slain from the foundation of the world" (Rev. 13:8 KJV). God has never been caught off guard by mankind's failures—and that includes yours!

Years ago, I said to the Lord, "I wouldn't choose to have children if I knew ahead of time they were going to rebel, betray, and dishonor me. I would be much happier without that type of child! Why, then, did You create us?"

He spoke this clear word to me: "My plan was to prove to mankind that My love would withstand every resistance. I allowed My love to be tested so that you would know it would always stand and never be withdrawn. I am Love. When anyone chooses to come into relationship with Me, they will never, ever need to doubt My love for them. Knowing I passed every test, they will feel completely secure—and that is My desire."

That's how much He loves you. Isn't it amazing? "Behold, what manner of love" is this (1 John 3:1 KJV)?

The Cross and the Covenant

God's plan is for you to have an eternal relationship with Him that is established through a covenant. A covenant is a legally binding agreement between two people or parties. For a covenant to work, there must be absolute integrity in the making and the keeping of all its terms. Entering into a covenant with a person of integrity gives you a sense of protection, a sense of security.

The marriage covenant is supposed to be like that. When you vow to be faithful, care for, and honor one another, you should feel a sense of belonging and oneness with each other. That is the purpose of covenant. It legally secures the relationship.

Mankind does not have a history of being covenant keepers, and so the very thing that should offer security is making many feel insecure. Some don't even bother getting married anymore, because they think it might last or it might not. That is one reason why there is so much family breakdown these days. There are broken covenants everywhere, evidenced by the high divorce rate in our nation. God, however, is a covenant-keeping God. He is full of integrity and always keeps the terms of the covenant He makes.

The original use of the word *covenant* meant "where the blood flows." Ancient covenants always set terms and exchanged names, weapons, and resources. Those covenants were almost always consummated through the mingling of blood. A covenant meal was served at the end of the ceremony and a celebration of the union commenced.

The marriage covenant is a blood covenant much like this. We make our vows before witnesses (an exchanging of terms), we exchange names (the bride usually takes her husband's name), and we exchange our resources (the assets of one legally become the other's, in most cases). The marriage is then consummated through the sexual act, which breaks the hymenal membrane (the shedding of blood).

God's covenant plan for His relationship with man was a blood covenant through Christ's blood shed for us at the cross. He set the terms (through the Old Testament Law and prophets) and then defined a name exchange (Jesus said, "Ask in My name," John 14:13), a weapons exchange (Jesus' weapons and armor are ours), and a resource exchange (all our needs are met through Him).

In ancient civilizations, a representative of one tribe would cut a covenant with a representative of another tribe. When the two leaders cut a covenant on behalf of their people, their entire tribe enjoyed the benefits of the covenant. This is what Christ did for us when he represented mankind in a covenant with God. Jesus Christ was—and is—our covenant representative and leader. It is His responsibility as our covenant representative to keep all the terms for us. In exchange, we receive all the covenant blessings. Wow!

The Amazing Good News!

What I'm about to share with you is amazing. God desired to make a covenant with man that would secure us in relationship with Him for all eternity. However, He knew that, once mankind fell, we would never be able to keep a covenant. It was impossible because we became filled with a sin nature. To fulfill the covenant terms, God required a sinless representative for man who would keep all the conditions, but there was not a sinless person to be found. As a result, He chose to fill that position Himself. He chose to take our place in covenant by becoming a man. Jesus, being both Man and God, was then in reality cutting a covenant with Himself. This is how God could cut an eternal, unbreakable, unfailing covenant with man. Jesus, who was fully God, left heaven and came into the sinful world as a man in order to fulfill this plan.

Many Christians don't understand this. I pray the light will go on for you today, because this truth is glorious. When you understand, you will worship and serve Him in full abandonment for all He has done. God loves you so very much. He desires relationship with you even more than you desire relationship with Him. He knew you couldn't keep a covenant, so He determined to become man and fulfill both sides of the covenant Himself. Jesus, the Son of God and Son of Man, made a covenant to include you in eternal relationship because you couldn't do it.

When He came as a man, He had to fulfill all of man's covenant terms that were laid out in Old Testament Law. If He failed to fulfill every point of the Law or if He gave in to temptation just once, He would not qualify to keep the covenant on man's behalf. This would have been devastating for us but there was an even greater risk for Him. Jesus is referred to in Scripture as "the last Adam" (see 1 Cor. 15:45). The first Adam was a perfect man before the fall. He was made in God's image and likeness. When he fell into temptation, the rule and dominion that had been given to him was surrendered over to satan. Romans 6:16 teaches that when we submit ourselves to sin, we become sin's slave. That is what happened to Adam when he submitted to satan's temptation, and that is what would have happened to the last Adam (Jesus) too, if He fell into even the slightest temptation. Only pure love would be willing to take a risk like that.

Jesus the Man

Just like the first Adam, Jesus was of man's nature, yet without sin. He was to fulfill man's requirement in covenant with man's power and capabilities. The Holy Spirit came upon Him to empower Him, just like the Holy Spirit empowers you today. Through the power of the Holy Spirit, the man Jesus remained sinless throughout His entire life on the earth. You need to understand that He resisted sin in man's strength, with the power of the Holy Spirit helping Him. You better believe that there was a huge wrestling in His soul against sin, even though He was perfect and without sin in His nature. He had to wrestle, just like the first Adam, because, in order to restore mankind to its rightful relationship with God, He had to secure the victory as a man. Ultimately, Jesus Christ, at the end of His "covenant course," would be acknowledged not only as perfect God but also as a perfect Man who would sit on a throne at the right hand of God. All things in Heaven and in earth would ultimately be summed up in Him.

It was not easy for Christ to resist sin. In fact, at one point His resistance against the temptations was so grueling that He sweat drops of blood (see Luke 22:44). He did it in man's power for you so you wouldn't have to do it—because you couldn't do it. Everything required for mankind to enter covenant with God was fulfilled through the man Jesus Christ. Jesus fulfilled all the Law and the prophets (see Luke 24:44).

Jesus Counts the Cost

I wonder if, before the foundation of the world, Jesus had to ask Himself, "How big is My love? Am I willing to perform acts of love, kindness, and mercy for people who don't even desire Me? Am I able to love so deeply that I would actually become sin for those whom I love? Am I willing to taste death for them?" He counted the cost and made a love choice with you in mind, saying, "Oh, yes! You are worth everything to Me. I will gladly leave Heaven and pay the price...with joy."

Jesus Arrives on Earth

Mary, a young virgin, conceived Jesus by the power of the Holy Spirit. She and Joseph traveled to Bethlehem where Mary went into labor. There was no available lodging so Mary gave birth in an animal's stable and laid baby Jesus in a feeding trough. What kind of treatment was this for man's Savior? No palace, no special treatment, and hardly anyone even discerned who He was (see Luke 1–2).

He had to start passing love tests right away. If He had been offendable, He could have thought, "Well, that's it; I'm going back to Heaven. I tried to do something nice for you, but you treated Me like an animal and threw Me into a feeding trough." Jesus, however, did not take offense but, in tremendous humility, passed the love test. Even though He was worthy of the most extravagant treatment, He didn't demand it or expect it. He came to serve.

Herod even tried to have Him killed when He was a baby (see Matt. 2:16), but Jesus never stopped loving. He never withdrew love and never lost faith. What would you do if your only motivation was to help people and, all of a sudden, they're trying to kill you? You'd probably say something like, "I don't need you. I'll go somewhere else." But Jesus had a different heart.

His Ministry Begins

His childhood passed, and His ministry began. He taught in the synagogues as a rabbi. The religious leaders examined His teachings carefully. They knew the Scriptures and were considered experts in the Word of God and doctrine. Jesus, however, is true doctrine. He is the living Word. He is true theology; and yet, He was called a blasphemer and a heretic by these very leaders. They attempted to bring legal charges against Him (see Matt. 22; Mark 3; John 8). This is the way they treated the true God.

How would you feel if you were God? There you are, teaching truth right from Heaven. You're speaking truth—because you are truth—and the people you came to save are saying, "You're a liar. You're a deceiver. You're a heretic. You're teaching us false doctrine. You're demonized." Character assaults like this are much worse than simply saying, "Your theology is off."

I've experienced a little of that resistance myself, and I must say those times were brutal. Everything in me wanted to withdraw. Jesus, however, never withdrew love from us, not for a moment. Each time He was opposed or mistreated by man, His love once again passed the test. He said, "I will never withdraw love, and I will never stop believing in what can happen in your life." He kept consistent in faith and love through all the mistreatment.

Jesus chose first 12 disciples and then 72 more. He poured His time and life into them by giving, teaching, and mentoring, day in and day out. Many others also followed His ministry. His own didn't always treat Him well, but even with all the disappointments He suffered, He never wavered in His commitment to them.

Love's Greatest Tests

The Garden of Gethsemane

One of Christ's most excruciating struggles was in Gethsemane (*Gethsemane* means "the oil press"). He faced every temptation that man would ever encounter. Strong forces of hell were spiritually assaulting Him. As we established earlier, Jesus had to resist sin as a man—in the same strength as the first Adam. You were in His heart the entire time He was wrestling against temptation. The pressure was so great against His soul that He sweat blood in His resistance against sin (see Luke 22:44). With every drop of blood that pushed through His bursting capillaries He was saying, "For you, I will resist. No matter what it feels like. No matter how excruciating it is. My emotions are being rung out beyond explanation but it's all for you. It's all for you."

I've faced some grueling spiritual battles and have engaged in warfare with powerful demonic entities. Although these seasons were unbearably painful, they were nothing at all in comparison to what Jesus experienced. I am a little aware, however, of the crushing feeling that pressures your emotions and your mind during such times. In the midst of this type of battle it is essential to keep focused, because all you have is the Word of God to stand on. Everything else that is going on in your life seems contrary to the truth, and there's just one point of choice: "I will stand on Your Word, Lord, no matter what. I will trust my soul into Your keeping." It is all you have.

At the end of these battles, your emotions, your thinking processes, and even your physical body are weakened, fatigued, and fragile. At times during these intense battles, I had to draw strength from God to even breathe. The impact of such warfare is excruciating; I can't even find words to describe it. What I experienced, however, is still nothing in comparison to the pressure that Jesus experienced.

What was it like for Jesus when He had the hordes of hell trying to take Him out? What motivated Him to stand through this agony? God didn't need to put Himself in this position. Do you know why He did? It was His love for you. He said, "I'm doing this to fulfill your covenant requirements." He loves you that much.

Just for a moment, forget about everyone else on the face of the earth. If you alone were left, He'd do it all over again. In the midst of Gethsemane's agony, you were in His vision. The thought of having you with Him for all eternity was His motivation to continue. Your face gave Him the strength to endure.

Betrayed by a Friend

When Jesus departed from the garden, He was weak and

exhausted. Judas, one of His 12 disciples, approached Him, betraying Him with a kiss. Even though Jesus knew Judas would betray Him, He continued to call Him "friend." He said, "Friend, do what you have come for" (Matt. 26:50).

Betrayal is very painful. If you have been betrayed, you know how difficult it is on your emotions, but even betrayal could not make Jesus withdraw love or friendship. There is nothing you can do to make Him withdraw His love. You can treat God terribly; You can tell Him to leave you alone, but He will never withdraw love from you. He'll continue to say, "I love you."

Abandoned and Denied

I can't imagine what it would feel like to be in a ferocious spiritual battle and then experience betrayal by a close friend and coworker. To top it all off, though, all His followers fled when He was arrested. When you're in a hard place, being falsely accused, you just want someone, even if it's only one, to stand with you. "Is there one who will just come to My side right now? Is there one who will believe in Me? Is there one who will defend Me?" Jesus did not even have one. His own disciples, whom He had poured Himself into for three years, all fled in fear of their reputations being destroyed.

As Jesus was led away, He heard Peter, one of His closest disciples, swearing, "I do not know Him" (Luke 22:57). Oh, how painful it must have been for Jesus when He heard that denial. He knew prophetically that Peter would do this, but foreknowledge doesn't ease the emotional devastation when it actually happens.

"Peter, I need you right now. Are you so afraid for your own life that you wouldn't even admit you know Me? Peter, look into my eyes and see My pain; see My love. You have denied Me, but You cannot make Me withdraw love from you."

His Trial

False witnesses were paid to testify against Jesus in court. That is harsh! When you know someone is lying about you, the natural tendency is to immediately defend yourself. Isaiah 53:7 reveals, though, that Jesus was like a lamb led to the slaughter, silent before His shearers, not opening His mouth in His own defense. He had purposed in His heart to offer unconditional love and mercy to the lying witnesses. "You can line your pockets with filthy lucre, but you cannot make Me withdraw My love from you."

They stripped Him naked, placed a crown of thorns on His head, and mocked Him openly. Even though you and I were not yet created, we were there, hidden in the heart of depraved humanity. We might think that we would never hurt or deny Him, but, like Peter we might not understand the weakness of our own flesh. It is probable that each of us would have done the same thing.

Christ's love was being severely tested by humankind. You and I have put His love to the test many times, and yet He has never abandoned us, and neither has He withdrawn love. He never will.

Beaten and Scourged

Jesus was beaten, spit upon, and mocked (see Matt. 27). His face was violently struck, apparently making Him unrecognizable. Again, with every cruel punch, His response was only love as He gazed into the eyes of His afflicters.

He was brutally scourged with a whip that had nine leather

strips. At the end of each strip were little pieces of sharp metal or bone. Each stroke provided nine lashings. It was a common belief that forty lashes would bring death. Under Roman laws He might have received even more. History reveals that His flesh was literally ripped open and that His innards were exposed. Every time the razor-sharp edge of the whip dug into His flesh, you were in His heart. Your face was constantly before Him. You were the reason He could endure such hostility. Looking into the face of those who were cruelly scourging Him, He would have said once again, "You cannot make Me withdraw My love." He would have assured you, too, if it was your hand holding the scourge.

Crucified

Jesus carried the heavy wooden cross that was heaved onto His back. Weakened with pain, He staggered up to Calvary's hill. An angry mob followed Him, mocking, ridiculing, and shouting, "Crucify Him. Crucify Him" (see Matt. 27; Mark 15; Luke 23; John 19). They nailed His hands and feet to the cross and hung Him between two guilty criminals. They were crucifying an innocent man.

To many, it looked like Jesus' life was being taken. It appeared that Jesus was defeated, but His life wasn't taken—it was given. The devil did not take Jesus' life. The false witnesses did not take His life. The Jews did not kill Him. The Romans did not kill Him. You did not kill Him. No one killed Him. He freely gave His life. When you see Jesus hanging on the cross, you see love Himself hanging there— a free gift of love—love that had been completely proven and tested against everything that could possibly oppose or destroy it.

Love Himself was on that cross, stripped naked and humiliated, hanging there in agonizing pain. In the midst of this agony, one of the thieves asked to be saved. Jesus didn't hesitate. In His greatest point of need, He continued to pour Himself out. He could have said, "What do you mean you want a favor from Me? Really? I don't deserve to be here, and you do. Forget it, it's too late!"

Jesus wasn't, and isn't, like that. He proved His love once again, "Of course, I will save you. In fact, today I'll do it, and you will be with Me in paradise. You will see the glory of My salvation" (see Luke 23:43).

Looking down from His cross, Jesus saw a mass of people—a crowd that delighted to watch Him die. "If You are the Son of God, come down from the cross" (Matt. 27:40). His merciful, loving retaliation was, "Father, forgive them; for they do not know what they are doing" (Luke 23:34).

Can you imagine? We sometimes find it difficult to forgive those who hurt or offend us. Consider Jesus: a mass of angry people rallied against Him, and you were there too—all humanity was. Oh yes, He saw your face in the crowd that day. We all sinned against Him, and yet He said, "Father, forgive them all." He forgave all the sins of mankind right at that point. He cancelled the debt of sin. Only pure Love Himself can do that.

He went even further and actually became mankind's sin. Jesus chose to become sin (see 2 Cor. 5:21). He chose to have your sin poured into Him so that He could pour His righteousness into you. He chose to become something abhorrent that would be judged so that you would be free from judgment.

Have you ever been mistreated, taken advantage of, or sinned against? Doesn't it give you a great feeling to see the offender punished, knowing they're getting what they deserve? But Jesus' heart was different. He said, "No, I'll take the punishment for your sin. I'll take full responsibility. You can go free."

A number of years ago, I was on the mission field. I misjudged a particular situation and consequently made some bad decisions. My actions seriously hurt some individuals. When I finally saw the situation clearly, I was terribly grieved, overwhelmed, and deeply ashamed. I thought I should have known better, I shouldn't have done that. It was difficult for me to believe that I hadn't seen the situation through eyes of wisdom in the first place. I asked for forgiveness from one individual who was particularly wounded through the process, but that person refused to extend the undeserved mercy that I desperately needed.

For years afterward, I had a very difficult time forgiving myself. One day, I was crying out to the Lord in prayer, "Don't let my failure continue to hurt them. Don't let it ruin their lives." I felt terrible to the very core of my being.

The Lord spoke very soberly to me. "You didn't commit that sin. You didn't make that mistake. I did."

"What? No, Lord! You never did that. I'm the one who did it."

"I did it," He insisted.

"Jesus, no, You didn't. You are perfect—and You have never wronged anyone, ever!"

He tenderly responded, "I bore your mistake on the cross 2,000 years ago. I chose to take full responsibility for this mistake so that you may go free. I have even borne the judgment for it. You are free! I became this sin for you, and in exchange, I have given you righteousness. This has all been paid in full. If there is any further problem, that hurting individual will need to come to Me. You have been totally released and fully justified. You never did it!"

I burst into tears, tears of gratitude that flowed from deep inside my being. How can I not love a God who showed that much mercy? He clearly revealed to me that day that this is what He's done for us all. This is what is called "substitution." He literally took our judgment and, in exchange, gave us His life and righteousness. Oh my, can we fully grasp this?

For All People and for All Time

God's love for us today is no different than it was for the sinful crowd at the foot of the cross 2,000 years ago. He performed an eternal exchange, saying, "It is no longer you who sinned, but Me. I have become your sin. I have paid the penalty. I have taken full responsibility. It is no longer your issue." Love laid down His life for you. You are free!

Dying in Faith

Gazing at you through the portals of time, Jesus died on the cross in love and in faith. He gave up the ghost and cried out, "It is finished" (John 19:30). Helpless, but remaining in faith, He entrusted His life into the hands of His Father. When He became your sin, He had no power to raise Himself from the dead. God planned

Christ's resurrection before the foundation of the world. And Jesus believed Him.

After His death, Jesus descended into the lower parts of the earth (see Eph. 4:9). On the third day, His Heavenly Father raised Him from the dead. Mary and the other women, the disciples, and many others literally saw Him walking the earth following His resurrection (see Acts 1:3). Oh yes, He is the Resurrection and the Life—the firstborn from the dead! When He was raised from the dead, He took the keys of death and of hell (see Rev. 1:18). He stripped the devil of his authority and made an open show of him. Oh, what an eternal victory!

Jesus Christ is forever the Resurrection and the Life. Jesus has invited everyone into eternal relationship with God through simply receiving Him as Savior by faith. All the work for mankind's redemption has been completed in Christ—finished! He did it all for us. The only thing left for us to do is to simply believe. Humankind's identity is found in Jesus—the One who accomplished everything for us. No man can boast in his own ability to save himself. Jesus fully paid the debt that we could not pay. He fully accomplished the work that we could not do. All glory to Him!

Jesus walked the earth for 40 days after His resurrection from the dead and then gloriously ascended to Heaven. He is forever seated at the right hand of God, far above all principalities, powers, and every name that is named (see Eph. 1:20-22). We are seated with Jesus in the heavenly places when we receive Him as our Savior (see Eph. 2:6). Our life is hidden with God in Christ (see Col. 3:3).

Sealed in the Covenant

Everyone who believes in Christ has the gift of everlasting life, His abundant life. Everyone who believes in Him is forever sealed into covenant, a legally binding love agreement between God and man. This covenant is an eternal covenant. It is impossible for it to be broken, because it is between Jesus-Man and Jesus-God. Jesus won our place for us through His own sinless life. When you believe in Him, you are saved from the separation from God that sin creates. Your identity as a Kingdom child is not in your own ability to accomplish anything. It is in His completed work—His ability—past tense. It is done! It is finished! In fact, if we were to be absolutely honest right now, you are an utter failure outside of Christ. It is impossible for you to please God in your own strength—absolutely impossible! The only way anyone can please God is by believing in Christ.

The arms of Jesus are open to all sinners. If you receive Jesus as Savior, then your identity is in Him. You are in Christ, a brand new creation. You are eternally one with Him. It is simple faith that connects you to this glorious eternal salvation. That's all you have to do—simply believe. That's it. That's all. Ephesians 2:8-9 says, "For by grace you have been saved through faith; and that not of yourselves, it is the gift of God; not as a result of works, so that no one may boast."

What is this grace that saves us? It is His divine influence in your life. It is His choice to accomplish everything for you. It is His work of favor over you—undeserved favor. You don't deserve it; I don't deserve it. No one does. It's undeserved, unmerited favor. It's His influence that comes upon your heart. You have been saved by grace through faith.

Simple faith is what connects you to the glorious, finished work of the cross. When you make this "faith connection," you become a brand new creation. Second Corinthians 5:17 (NKJV) states, "Therefore, if anyone is in Christ, he is a new creation; old things have passed away; behold, all things have become new."

Ah, what a glorious life we have been given in Christ—a brand new life; eternal relationship with God Himself. Christ did all this for you! You see how precious you are? God loves you with an everlasting love...He really does!

Perhaps you have just read through this little booklet and your heart is longing to become God's child. It's simple. The following is a little prayer. If it represents your desire, why don't you go ahead and pray it from your heart? God will hear you. His gift of life and love will enter you and your journey begins!

Heavenly Father,

I come to You, acknowledging Your love for me. I believe that You sent Your Son Jesus Christ to die on the cross for my sins. I believe He paid the full penalty for my sins and has offered me eternal life. I accept the gift of Your love. Jesus, come into my heart right now and make me a brand new person within. Thank you for forgiving my sin and for giving me eternal life. I thankfully receive Your precious gift of love. Amen.

Your New Life Begins

When you receive Jesus as your personal Savior by faith, His life enters your spirit. You are now what Scripture calls *born again* (read John 3:1-9). You have Christ's brand new life inside you. His purity, love, peace, truth, and blessings are now inside your spirit. You are beautiful and perfect within.

Just like a newborn baby needs nourishment and care, so do new babies in the Lord. The Bible is full of truth that is like fresh milk and food for you. As you read it each day, it will nourish you and reveal wonderful things about God's love and His ways.

You will also want to meet some other Christians who understand the love of God. Fellowship with other followers of Jesus is great fun. Take some time and visit some churches in your area. Christ's Holy Spirit dwells within you, and He will direct you to a good fellowship if you ask Him to.

As a child of your Heavenly Father, you are invited to communicate with Him through prayer. Prayer is easy—you simply share your heart with Him. He loves to answer your desires. Some good teaching on prayer will help you to grow in understanding and practicing the many different ways that you can communicate with God. Prayer is very fulfilling and powerful.

All of God's goodness belongs to you when you are in Christ... so imbibe of it all. You have been called to full and glorious life in Jesus. Enjoy!

Decree (Booklet)

Decree Booklet by Patricia King—permission granted to print.
Copyright 2003, Patricia King.

Dear friends:

The powerful Word of God is well able to profoundly influence your life. In Christ you have an eternal and unbreakable covenant. All of His promises are "*Yes*" and "*Amen*" (2 Corinthians 1:20 NKJV) to you!

Daily confession of the Word will strengthen your inner man and prepare you for every good work. The following are some reasons why the confession of the Word is found to be powerful in our lives.

The Word of God:

- Is eternal in the heavens—*Matthew 24:35*
- Will not return void—*Isaiah 55:11*
- Frames the will of God—*Hebrews 11:3*
- Dispatches angels—*Psalm 103:20*
- Brings light into darkness—*Psalm 119:130*
- Is a lamp unto our feet and a light unto our path—*Psalm 119:105*
- Secures blessings—*Ephesians 1:3; 2 Peter 1:3*
- Is seed—*Mark 4*
- Is our weapon of warfare—*Ephesians 6; 2 Corinthians 10:3-5*
- Pulls down mind-sets—*2 Corinthians 10:3-5*
- Creates—*Romans 4:17*
- Sanctifies—*John 17:17; Ephesians 5:26*
- Strengthens the spirit man—*Ephesians 3:16*
- Ensures answers to prayer—*John 15:7*

May you truly enjoy a season of strengthening and may you be forever established in the manifestation of His glorious Word.

Visit our Website at www.extremeprophetic.com or contact us by phone (toll-free for Canada and the U.S.A.) 1-866-765-9286 or 250-765-9286.

In His victorious service with you,

Patricia King

Prayer of Dedication

Dear Heavenly Father,

I dedicate myself to You this day, in spirit, soul, and body. Convict me of any thought, word, or deed that has been displeasing to You. I ask for cleansing from all sin, according to the promise in Your Word that if I confess my sin then You will be faithful to forgive me and to cleanse me from all unrighteousness (1 John 1:9).

As I confess and decree Your Word, may Your Holy Spirit help me to be a passionate worshiper, a lover of truth, and a faithful child who brings pleasure to Your righteous heart.

May I experience spiritual strengthening through the power of Your Word, for Your Word does not return void but accomplishes everything it is sent to do.

Grant unto me a spirit of wisdom and of revelation in the knowledge of Christ, for the glory of Your Name and Kingdom.

In Jesus' name, I pray. Amen.

With my whole heart I have sought You; Oh, let me not wander from Your commandments! Your word I have hidden in my heart, That I might not sin against You. (Psalm 119:10-11 NKJV).

Decree

Praise and Worship

Heavenly Father, I worship You in spirit and in truth. Along with the host of Heaven, I declare:

Holy, holy, holy, Lord God Almighty,
Who was and is and is to come!
You are worthy O Lord, to receive glory and honor and
*   power;*
For You created all things and by Your will they exist.
Blessing and honor and glory and power
Be to Him who sits on the throne,
And to the Lamb, forever, and ever!
Holy, holy, holy is the LORD of hosts;
The whole earth is full of His glory!

You, O Lord are sitting on Your throne, high and lifted up, and the train of Your robe fills the temple. I ascribe greatness to You, for You are my God and my Rock. Your work is perfect, and all Your ways are just. You are a God of faithfulness and without injustice; righteous and upright are You.

I love You, O Lord my God, with all my heart, mind, and strength. You are the Lord, and there is no other. There is no God besides You. I glory in Your holy name, and my heart rejoices in You. I will seek Your face evermore! I bless You, O Lord, my God. You are very great. You are clothed with honor and majesty.

While I live, I will praise You. I will sing praises to You while I have my being. The high praises of God will be in my mouth and a two-edged sword in my hand.

Praise the Lord!
Praise the Lord from the heavens;
Praise Him in the heights!
Praise Him, all His angels;
Praise Him, all His hosts!
Praise Him, sun and moon;
Praise Him, all you stars of light!
Praise Him, you heavens of heavens,
And you waters above the heavens!

SCRIPTURAL REFERENCES: John 4:24; Revelation 4:8,11; 5:13, NKJV; Isaiah 6:3 NKJV; Isaiah 6:1; Deuteronomy 32:3-4; Isaiah 45:5; Psalm 105:3-4; 104:1; 146:2; 149:6; 148:1-4 NKJV.

Decree

Everlasting Love

The Lord loves me with an everlasting love and has promised to give me a future and a hope. With loving-kindness has drawn me unto Himself. I look carefully at the manner of love the Father has poured out upon me. It is through this love that He has called me to be His dear child. I am completely and fully accepted in Him, my God and Savior.

Nothing can separate me from the love of God that is in Christ my Lord—not tribulation or distress; not persecution, famine, or nakedness; not peril, sword, angels, principalities, powers, death, or life; neither things present nor things to come—absolutely nothing can separate me from the love of God which is in Christ Jesus my Lord.

God's love toward me is patient and kind. His love for me bears all things, believes all things, hopes all things, and endures all things. His love will never fail. His love for me is so rich that He gave His only begotten Son. Because of this, I will never perish but have everlasting life with Him. As a result of God's great love for me, I have an unbreakable, eternal covenant with Him. Through this covenant of love, He has put His laws within my heart and written His commandments upon my mind.

I have been invited to the Lord's banqueting table, and His banner over me is love! His love is better than the choicest of wines. Through His intimate love, He draws me and invites me to follow after Him. I am fair and pleasant unto Him. I am rooted and grounded in His love, well able to comprehend with all believers the width and length and depth and height of His unfailing love. I have been called to know this rich love that surpasses knowledge, so that I may be filled with all the fullness of God. I truly am the object of His deepest love and affection!

SCRIPTURAL REFERENCES: Jeremiah 31:3; 1 John 3:1; Ephesians 1:6; Romans 8:38-39; 1 Corinthians 13:4,7-8; John 3:16; Hebrews 8:10; Song of Solomon 1:2,4; 2:4; Ephesians 1:18-19)

Decree

Who I Am in Christ

I am a child of God; God is spiritually my Father. (See Romans 8:14-15; Galatians 3:26, 4:6; Colossians 1:12.)

I am a new creation in Christ; old things have passed away and all things have become new. (See 2 Corinthians 5:17.)

I am in Christ. (See Ephesians 1; Galatians 3:26,28.)

I am an heir with the Father and a joint heir with Christ. (See Galatians 4:6-7; Romans 8:17.)

I am reconciled to God and am an ambassador of reconciliation for Him. (See 2 Corinthians 5:18-19.)

I am a saint. (See Ephesians 1:1; 1 Corinthians 1:2; Philippians 1:1; Colossians 1:2.)

I am God's workmanship, created in Christ for good works. (See Ephesians 2:10.)

I am a citizen of Heaven. (See Ephesians 2:19; Philippians 3:20.)

I am a member of Christ's body. (See 1 Corinthians 12:27.)

I am united to the Lord and am one spirit with Him. (See 1 Corinthians 6:17.)

I am the temple of the Holy Spirit. (See 1 Corinthians 3:16; 6:19.)

I am a friend of Christ. (See John 15:15.)

I am a slave of righteousness. (See Romans 6:18.)

I am the righteousness of God in Christ (See 2 Corinthians 5:21.)

I am enslaved to God. (See Romans 6:22.)

I am chosen and ordained by Christ to bear fruit. (See John 15:16.)

I am a prisoner of Christ. (See Ephesians 3:1; 4:1.)

I am righteous and holy. (See Ephesians 4:24.)

I am hidden with Christ in God. (See Colossians 3:3.)

I am the salt of the earth. (See Matthew 5:13.)

I am the light of the world. (See Matthew 5:14.)

I am part of the true vine. (See John 15:1-2.)

I am filled with the divine nature of Christ and escape the corruption that is in the world through lust. (See 2 Peter 1:4.)

I am an expression of the life of Christ. (See Colossians 3:4.)

I am chosen of God, holy, and dearly loved. (See Colossians 3:12; 1 Thessalonians 1:4.)

I am a child of light. (See 1 Thessalonians 5:5.)

I am a partaker of a heavenly calling. (See Hebrews 3:1.)

I am more than a conqueror through Christ. (See Romans 8:37.)

I am a partaker with Christ and share in His life. (See Hebrews 3:14.)

I am one of God's living stones, being built up in Christ as a spiritual house. (See 1 Peter 2:5.)

I am a chosen generation, a royal priesthood, a holy nation. (See 1 Peter 2:9.)

I am the devil's enemy. (See 1 Peter 5:8.)

I am born again by the Spirit of God. (See John 3:3-6.)

I am an alien and stranger to this world. (See 1 Peter 2:11.)

I am a child of God who always triumphs in Christ and releases His fragrance in every place. (See 2 Corinthians 2:14.)

I am seated in heavenly places in Christ. (See Ephesians 2:6.)

I am saved by grace. (See Ephesians 2:8.)

I am a recipient of every spiritual blessing in the heavenly places in Christ. (See Ephesians 1:3.)

I am redeemed by the blood of the Lamb. (See Revelation 5:9.)

I am part of the Bride of Christ and am making myself ready for Him. (See Revelation 19:7.)

I am a true worshiper who worships the Father in spirit and in truth. (See John 4:24.)

Decree

Victory

I am a child of the living God. I am an heir of God and a joint heir with Jesus Christ. I am a new creation in Jesus; old things have passed away and all things have become new. I am a chosen generation, a royal priest-hood, a holy nation.

I am not under guilt or condemnation. I refuse discouragement, because it is not of God. God is the God of all encouragement. There is therefore now no condemnation for those who are in Christ Jesus. The law of the Spirit of life in Christ Jesus has set me free from the law of sin and death. I do not listen to satan's accusations for he is a liar, the father of lies. I gird up my loins with truth. Sin does not have dominion over me.

I flee from temptation but if I do sin, I have an advocate with the Father who is Jesus Christ. I confess my sins and forsake them, and God is faithful and just to forgive me and to cleanse me from all unrighteousness. I am cleansed by the blood of the Lamb. I am an over-comer, because of the blood of Jesus and the word of my testimony.

No weapon that is formed against me shall prosper, and I shall confute every tongue that rises up against me in judgment. My mind is renewed by the Word of God.

The weapons of my warfare are not carnal but mighty through God to the pulling down of strong-holds. I cast down imaginations and every high thing that exalts itself against the knowledge of Christ. I bring every thought captive into obedience to the Truth.

I am accepted in the Beloved. Greater is He that is in me than he that is in the world. Nothing can separate me from the love of God which is in Christ Jesus my Lord. I am the righteousness of God in Christ Jesus. I am not the slave of sin, but of righteousness. I continue in His Word. I know the truth and the Truth sets me free. Because Christ has set me free, I am free indeed. I have been delivered out of the domain of darkness and am now abiding in the Kingdom of God.

I am not intimidated by the enemy's lies. He is defeated. For this purpose Christ came into the world, to destroy the works of the evil one. I submit to God and resist the devil. The enemy flees from me in terror, because the Lord lives mightily in me. I give the devil no opportunity. I give no place to fear in my life. God has not given me a spirit of fear but of love, of power, and of a sound mind. Terror shall not come near me, because the Lord is the strength of my life and He always causes me to triumph in Christ Jesus.

In Christ, I am the head and not the tail. I am above and not beneath. A thousand shall fall at my side and ten thousand at my right hand, yet none shall touch me. I am seated with Christ in the heavenly places, far above all principalities and powers. I have been given power to tread upon serpents and scorpions and over all the power of the enemy, and nothing shall injure me. No longer will the enemy oppress me. I defeat him by the authority that Christ has given me. I am more than a conqueror through Christ.

SCRIPTURAL REFERENCES: Romans 6:16; 8:1-2,17,32,37,39; 12:2; 2 Corinthians 2:14; 5:17,21; 10:3-5; 1 Peter 2:9; John 8:36,44; Ephesians 1:6,20-21; 4:27; 6:14; 1 John 1:9; 2:1; 3:8; Revelation 12:11; Isaiah 54:17; Colossians 1:13; James 4:7; 2 Timothy 1:7; Psalm 27:1; Deuteronomy 28:13; Psalm 9 1:7; Luke 10:19.

Decree

Wisdom

Jesus Christ has become wisdom, righteousness, sanctification, and redemption unto me. Because Christ dwells within me, I know wisdom and instruction. My God gives unto me a spirit of wisdom and of revelation in the knowledge of Christ. When I lack wisdom, I ask in faith and it is given to me generously. This is heavenly wisdom which is first pure, then peaceable, gentle, easily entreated, full of mercy and good fruits, unwavering, and without hypocrisy.

I discern the sayings of understanding, and I receive instruction in wise behavior, justice, and fairness. I walk in the fear of the Lord, which is the beginning of knowledge. Jesus pours out His spirit of wisdom upon me and makes His words of wisdom known to me.

I receive the sayings of wisdom, and I treasure the

commandments of the Lord within me. My ear is attentive to wisdom, and I incline my heart to understanding. I cry for discernment and lift my voice for understanding. I seek for wisdom as for silver and search for it as for hidden treasures. Because of this, I will discern the fear of the Lord and discover the knowledge of God. The Lord gives me wisdom.

From His mouth comes knowledge and understanding. He stores up sound wisdom for me. He is a shield to me, and He guards my paths with justice and preserves my way. Wisdom enters my heart and knowledge is pleasant to my soul. Discretion guards me, and understanding watches over me to deliver me from the way of evil.

I do not let kindness and truth leave me. I bind them around my neck and write them on the tablet of my heart, so that I find favor and good repute with God and man. I trust in the Lord with all my heart, and I do not lean on my own understanding. In all my ways I acknowledge Him, and He makes my paths straight. I am blessed, because I find wisdom and I gain understanding.

I have long, full life, because it is in wisdom's right hand, and I have the riches and honor that are in wisdom's left hand. Because I love wisdom, all my paths are peace and my ways pleasant. Wisdom is a tree of life to me, and I am blessed because I hold her fast. I inherit honor, because of my love for wisdom, and my dwelling is blessed.

I acquire wisdom and understanding. I do not forsake wisdom; therefore, wisdom is my guard. I love wisdom and am watched over. Because I prize and embrace wisdom, wisdom exalts and honors me. Wisdom places a garland of grace on my head and presents me with a crown of beauty. I call wisdom my sister and understanding my intimate friend.

Because I love wisdom, riches and honor are with me, enduring wealth and righteousness. Wisdom endows me with wealth and fills my treasuries. I listen to wisdom and daily watch at her gates. I eat wisdom's food and drink of the wine that she has mixed. I forsake folly and live. I proceed in the way of understanding. When I speak, I speak noble things, and the opening of my mouth produces right things. My mouth utters truth. All the utterances of my mouth are in righteousness, because I walk in the way of wisdom.

SCRIPTURAL REFERENCES: 1 Corinthians 1:30; Ephesians 1:17; James 1:5; 3:17; Proverbs 1:2-3,7,23; 2:1-12; 3; 4:5-9; 7:4; 8:6-8; 9:5-6.

Decree

Provision and Resource

I seek first the Kingdom of God and His righteousness, and all the things that I need are added unto me, for my Heavenly Father knows what I need even before I ask. I do not fear, for it is my Father's good pleasure to give me the Kingdom.

I acknowledge that all my needs are met according to God's riches in glory by Christ Jesus. Grace and peace are multiplied unto me through the knowledge of God and of Jesus my Lord. His divine power has given me all things that pertain unto life and godliness, through the knowledge of Him that has called me to glory and virtue. Blessed be the God and Father of my Lord Jesus Christ, who has blessed me with every spiritual blessing in the heavenly places in Christ. The Lord is a sun and a shield to me and will give me grace and glory. No good thing will He withhold from me as I walk uprightly.

I choose to sow bountifully; therefore, I will reap bountifully. I give to the Lord, to His people, and to the needy as I purpose in my heart to give. I do not give grudgingly or out of compulsion, for my God loves a cheerful giver. God makes all grace abound toward me; I always have enough for all things, so that I may abound unto every good work.

The Lord supplies seed for me to sow and bread for my food. He also supplies and multiplies my seed for sowing and increases the fruits of my righteousness. I am enriched in everything unto great abundance, which brings much thanksgiving to God.

I bring all my tithes into the Lord's storehouse, so that there is meat in His house. As a result, He opens up the windows of Heaven and pours out a blessing for me so that there is not room enough to contain it. He rebukes the devourer for my sake, so that he does not destroy the fruits of my ground and neither does my vine cast its grapes before the time. All the nations shall call me blessed, for I shall have a delightful life. I am blessed, because I consider the poor. Because I give freely to the poor, I will never want. My righteousness endures forever.

I remember the Lord my God, for it is He who gives me the power to make wealth, that He may confirm His covenant. Because Jesus Christ my Savior diligently listened to the voice of God and obeyed all the commandments, the Lord will set me high above all the nations of the earth and all the blessings in the Kingdom shall come upon me and overtake me. Christ became poor so that through His poverty I might become rich.

Jesus came so that I would have life in its abundance. I am very blessed and favored of God and have been called to be a blessing to others.

SCRIPTURAL REFERENCES: Matthew 6:33; Philippians 4:19; Luke 12:32; 2 Peter 1:2,3; Ephesians 1:3; Psalm 84:11; 2 Corinthians 8:9; 9:6-11; Psalm 41:1; Ps112:1a,9; Proverbs 28:27; Malachi 3:8-12; Deuteronomy 8:18; 28:1,22; John 10:10; Genesis 12:2.

Decree

For Christian Character

I am the light of the world. A city set on a hill cannot be hidden. I let my light so shine before men that they may see my good works and glorify my Father who is in Heaven. Grace and peace are multiplied to me through the knowledge of God and of Jesus my Lord. His divine power has granted me everything that pertains to life and to godliness.

He has given me exceeding great and precious promises. I live by these promises so that I might be a partaker of His divine nature, having escaped the corruption that is in the world through lust. Besides this, I give all diligence and add to my faith virtue, and to virtue knowledge, and to knowledge temperance, and to temperance patience, and to patience godliness. To godliness, I add brotherly kindness and to brotherly kindness love. As these things are in me and abounding, I shall never be barren nor unfruitful in the knowledge of my Lord Jesus.

I choose to walk worthy of the Lord in every respect, being fruitful in every good work and increasing in the knowledge of God. I give thanks to my Heavenly Father who has made me to be a partaker of the inheritance of the saints in light. He has delivered me from the power of darkness and has translated me to the Kingdom of

His dear Son, in whom I have redemption through His blood, even the forgiveness of sin.

I am an imitator of God, as a dear child. I walk in love. Fornication and all uncleanness and covetousness have no part in my life, neither filthiness nor coarse jesting nor foolish talking, which are not fitting, but rather the giving of thanks. I let no corrupt communication proceed out of my mouth, but only that which is edifying, that it may minister grace to the hearers. I will not grieve the Holy Spirit of God whereby I have been sealed unto the day of redemption.

I choose to walk in lowliness of mind and esteem others as better than myself. I look not to my own interests but also to the interests of others. I make myself of no reputation and take the form of a bondservant.

I wait for the Lord and let integrity and uprightness preserve me. Jesus is a buckler to me, because I walk uprightly. I dwell on those things that are true, honorable, right, pure, lovely, of good repute, excellent, and worthy of praise.

As a child of God, I am thoroughly furnished for every good work. I consider how to provoke others to love. I put on a heart of compassion, kindness, humility, gentleness, and patience, for I am God's workmanship, created in Christ Jesus for good deeds, which God prepared beforehand that I should walk in them.

I am patient and kind. I am not jealous. I do not brag and I am not arrogant. I do not act unbecomingly and do not seek my own way. I am not easily provoked and do not take into account a wrong suffered. I do not rejoice in unrighteousness, but rejoice with the truth. I bear all things, believe all things, hope all things, and endure all things. The love of Jesus in me does not fail.

SCRIPTURAL REFERENCES: Matthew 5:14-16; 2 Peter 1:2-8; Ephesians 2:10; 4:29-30; 5:1-5; Colossians 1:9-14; 3:12; Philippians 2:3-7; 4:8; 1 Corinthians 13:4-8; 2 Timothy 3:17; Hebrews 10:24.

Decree

For Spiritual Strength

I am strong in the Lord and in the strength of His might. I put on the full armor of God. In Christ I can do all things, because He strengthens me.

The Lord is my strength and my shield. My heart trusts in Him and I am helped; therefore my heart exults, and with my song I shall thank Him. He is my strength and my saving defense in time of trouble. The grace of the Lord Jesus Christ is with my spirit.

I build myself up in my holy faith, praying in the Holy Spirit. As I do this, I keep myself strong in the love of God. My God keeps me from falling and presents me faultless and blameless in the presence of my Heavenly Father with exceeding great joy.

My help comes from the Lord who made Heaven and earth. He will not allow my foot to slip, and He who keeps me will not slumber. The Lord is my keeper. The Lord is my shade on my right hand. The sun does not smite me by day nor the moon by night. The Lord protects me from all evil. He keeps my soul, and He guards my going out and my coming in, from this time forth and forever.

When I pass through the valley of weeping, the Lord makes it a spring for me. I go from strength to strength in the Lord. The Lord God is a sun and a shield to me. He gives me grace and glory and no good thing does He withhold from me. I am blessed, because I trust in Him.

My Heavenly Father grants unto me, according to the riches of His glory, the ability to be strengthened with power through His Spirit in my inner man, so that Christ may dwell in my heart through faith, and that I, being rooted and grounded in love, may be able to comprehend with all believers what is the breadth and length and height and depth and to know the love of Christ which surpasses knowledge, that I may be filled up to all the fullness of God.

I do not lose heart in doing good, for in due time I shall reap if I faint not. My eye is single, therefore my whole being is full of light. I am steadfast, immovable, always abounding in the work of the Lord, knowing that my toil is not in vain in the

Lord. God is my strong fortress and He sets me in His way.

By Him, I can run through a troop and I can leap over a wall. He is a shield, because I take refuge in Him. He makes my feet like hinds' feet and sets me on my high places. He trains my hands for battle so that my arms can bend a bow of bronze. He has given me the shield of His salvation, and His help and strength make me great. I pursue my enemies and destroy them, because the Lord has girded me with strength for battle.

The Lord gives me strength when I am weary, and when I lack might, He increases power. I wait on the Lord and renew my strength. I mount up with wings like eagles. I run and do not get tired; I walk and do not faint.

SCRIPTURAL REFERENCES: Ephesians 6:10; Philippians 4:13; Psalm 28:7-8; 37:39; 84:5-7,11; 121; Philippians 4:23; Jude 1:20-21,24; Ephesians 3:16-19; Galatians 6:7-9; Matthew 6:22; 1 Corinthians 15:58; 2 Samuel 22:30-40; Isaiah 40:29-31.

Decree

Empowered to Go

I receive power when the Holy Spirit comes upon me to be the Lord's witness, even unto the uttermost parts of the earth. In Jesus' name, I go into all the world to preach the gospel to every creature.

These signs follow me as I go, because I believe: In the name of Jesus, I cast out devils, I speak with new tongues, I take up serpents, and if I drink any deadly poison, it shall not harm me. When I lay hands on the sick, they shall recover. I go forth and preach everywhere, and the Lord confirms the Word I preach with signs that follow. When I go, I go in the fullness of the blessing of the gospel of Christ.

The works that Jesus does, I do also in His name, and even greater works I do, because He has gone to the Father. Greater is He that is in me than he that is in the world. Jesus has given me power over all the power of the enemy. He has given me power over unclean spirits to cast them out and has enabled me to heal all manner of sickness and all manner of disease.

As I go, I will preach, saying, "The Kingdom of Heaven is at hand." I will heal the sick, cleanse the lepers, raise the dead. I will cast out devils. Freely I have received, so I will freely give. The Lord grants me boldness to speak His Word. He stretches out His hand toward me to heal and that signs and wonders may be done through the name of Jesus Christ. His Spirit has been poured out upon me and I prophesy.

All power in Heaven and in earth has been given unto Jesus Christ. I will go in His name and teach all nations, baptizing them in the name of the Father, the Son, and the Holy Spirit. I will teach them to observe all things that Jesus has taught me. Jesus is with me, even unto the end of the world. He has called me to Himself and has given me power and authority over all devils and to cure diseases. He has sent me to preach the Kingdom of God and to heal the sick. As I go, Jesus prepares my way with His favor, for the Lord surrounds His righteous with favor as a shield. He sends His angels before me to watch over my ways and to bear me up lest I fall.

Like Jesus, I have been anointed with the Holy Spirit and with power. I go about doing good and healing all that are oppressed of the devil, for God is with me. He has anointed me to preach the gospel to the poor. He has sent me to proclaim release to the captives and recovery of sight to the blind, to set free all who are downtrodden, and to proclaim the favorable year of the Lord.

I arise and shine, because my light has come and the glory of the Lord has risen upon me. Darkness shall cover the earth and gross darkness the peoples, but the Lord has risen upon me and His glory appears upon me. Nations will come to my light in Christ and kings to the brightness of my rising.

My speech and my preaching is not with enticing words of man's wisdom but in the demonstration of the Spirit and of power, that the faith of those I preach to should not stand on the wisdom of men, but in the power of God for the Kingdom of God is not in word but in power.

The Lord grants unto me, according to His riches in glory, to be strengthened with might by His Spirit in my inner man, according to His glorious power, unto all patience and longsuffering with joy. I labor according to His power that works mightily within me.

I preach not myself but Christ Jesus as Lord and myself as a bondservant of Christ and His Body, for Jesus' sake. For God who said, "Light shall shine out of darkness," is the One who has shone in our hearts to give the light of the knowledge of the glory of God in the face of Christ. I have this treasure in an earthen vessel, that the surpassing greatness of the power may be of God and not of myself.

Now unto the King eternal, immortal, invisible, the only wise God, who is able to do exceedingly abundantly above all that I could ask or think, according to the power that works within me, be honor and glory forever and ever. Amen.

SCRIPTURAL REFERENCES: Acts 1:8; 10:38; Mark 16:15-21; Romans 15:29; John 14:12; 1 John 4:4; Luke 4:18; 10:1-2,19; Matthew 10:1,7; 28:18-20; Acts 4:29-30; 2:17-18; Isaiah 60:1-3; Psalm 5:12; 91:11; 1 Corinthians 2:4; 4:19; Ephesians 3:16,20; Colossians 1:11,29; 2 Corinthians 4:5-6; 1 Timothy 1:17.

Decree

Health and Healing

I praise the Lord with all that is within me and do not forget any of His benefits. He forgives all my sins and heals all my diseases; He redeems my life from the pit and crowns me with love and compassion. Jesus satisfies my desires with good things, so that my youth is renewed like the eagle's.

The Lord brings me to health and healing. He heals me and lets me enjoy abundant peace and security. The Sun of righteousness arises for me with healing in His wings, and I go out and leap like a calf released from the stall. Jesus bore my sins in His body on the cross, so that I might die to sin and live to righteousness. By His stripes I am healed. As my days are, so shall my strength be.

Jesus sent forth His Word and healed me; He rescued me from the grave. When I cry out, the Lord hears me; He delivers me from all my troubles. The Lord is close to me when I am broken-hearted and saves me when I am crushed in spirit. He has not given me a spirit of fear, but of love, power, and a sound mind.

At times I may have many troubles, but the Lord delivers me from them all; He protects all my bones; not one of them will be broken. I am like an olive tree flourishing in the house of God; I trust in God's unfailing love forever and ever.

When the Lord's servants lay hands on me I recover, and when I am sick I call for the elders who pray over me, anointing me with oil in the name of the Lord. The prayer of faith saves me, and the Lord raises me up.

The law of the spirit of life in Christ Jesus has set me free from the law of sin and death. Jesus is the Resurrection and the Life. Because I believe in Him, I will live for all eternity. In Christ I live and move and have my being.

Because I dwell in the shelter of the Most High and rest in the shadow of the Almighty, I will say of the Lord, "He is my refuge and my fortress, my God, in whom I trust." Surely He will save me from the fowler's snare and from the deadly pestilence. He covers me with His feathers, and under His wings I find refuge; His faithfulness is my shield and rampart. I do not fear the terror of night, nor the arrow that flies by day, nor the pestilence that stalks in the darkness, nor the plague that destroys at midday. A thousand may fall at my side, ten thousand at my right hand, but they will not come near me. I will only observe with my eyes and see the punishment of the wicked. Because I make the Most High my dwelling—even the Lord, who is my refuge—then no harm will befall me, no disaster will come near my tent. He will command his angels concerning me to guard me in all my ways; they will lift me up in their hands so that I will not strike my foot against a stone. I will tread upon the lion and the cobra; I will trample the great lion and the serpent. Because I love the Lord, He will rescue and protect me from all accident, harm, sickness, and disease. He is with me in trouble and delivers me. With long life He satisfies me and shows me His salvation.

Because I consider the poor, the Lord will deliver me in times of trouble. The Lord will protect me and keep me alive, and I shall be blessed upon the earth. He will not give me over to the desire of my enemies. The Lord will sustain me upon my sickbed; in my illness, He will restore me to health.

SCRIPTURE REFERENCES: Psalm 34:17-20; 41:1-3; 52:8; 103:1-3; 91; 107:20; Deuteronomy 33:25; Jeremiah 33:6; Malachi 4:2; 1 Peter 2:24; Deuteronomy 33:25; Romans 12:1; John 11:25-26; 2 Timothy 1:17; Mark 16:18; James 5:14-15.

Decree

For Business and the Workplace

In my business/workplace I am surrounded with favor as a shield. I arise and shine, for my light has come. The rich among the people entreat my favor. In Christ, I show no defect, but function in intelligence in every branch of wisdom, being endowed with understanding and discerning knowledge. The Lord gives me the knowledge of witty inventions and causes me to grow in wisdom, in stature and favor with God and man.

In my business/workplace, I am the head and not the tail. I am above and not beneath. The Lord commands blessings upon my business/workplace, and every project that I put my hands to prospers. He establishes my business and workplace as holy unto Himself.

My business/workplace does not submit to the Babylonian/world system, but instead submits to the Kingdom of God and His righteousness. The integrity of the Lord guides me in my business. The Lord looks upon my business/workplace with regard and makes it fruitful, multiplying its productivity.

No weapon formed against my business/workplace prospers. Every tongue that rises up against it in judgment I condemn. The Lord is a wall of fire around my business/workplace, and His glory is in the midst of it.

The Lord leads me by His presence, and He gives me rest. He makes goodness to pass before my business/workplace. His goodness and mercy follows me all the days of my life.

Peace, unity, love, integrity, honor, and servanthood are godly values that prevail in my business/workplace.

I decree that Jesus Christ is Lord over my life, business, and workplace!

SCRIPTURAL REFERENCES: Psalm 5:12; Isaiah 60:1; Psalm 45:12;

Daniel 1:4; Deuteronomy 28:1-13; Revelation 18:4; Proverbs 11:3: Leviticus 26:9; Isaiah 54:17; Zechariah 2:5; Exodus 33:14,19; Psalm 23:6.

Decree

For Family and Children

As for me and my family, we will serve the Lord. Because I believe in the Lord Jesus Christ, I shall be saved, and my entire house. Because I am a covenant child of God, my household is blessed. We have been blessed with every spiritual blessing in Christ. Blessings come upon us and overtake us.

My family, home, marriage, and children are blessed, and all that I put my hands to do. I am blessed coming in, and I am blessed going out. The Lord has established my household as a people for Himself. He causes us to abound in prosperity, in the offspring of our bodies and the offspring of our beasts and the produce of our ground. The Lord surrounds my family and entire household with favor as a shield. No good thing does He withhold from us. His banner is love, over my home, marriage, and family. No weapon formed against us as a family prospers. What the Lord has blessed, no man can curse. We abide in the shadow of the Almighty and no evil befalls us.

My children shall be mighty on the earth, for the generations of the upright are blessed. They shall be as signs and wonders in the earth.

My children will flourish like olive plants around my table. They are a gift from the Lord, and the fruit of the womb is my reward. My children are like arrows in the hand of a warrior. My sons in their youth are as grown-up plants and my daughters as corner pillars fashioned as for a palace.

Lord, Your covenant with me declares that Your Spirit which is upon me and Your words which You have put in my mouth shall not depart from my mouth, nor from the mouth of my children, nor from the mouth of my children's children. All my children shall be taught of the Lord, and great shall be their peace and prosperity. In righteousness they will be established, and they will be far from oppression. They will not be led into temptation, but they will know deliverance from evil. I confess that my children are pure in heart and therefore they shall see God. They hunger and thirst after righteousness, therefore they are filled. The Spirit of the Lord is poured out upon my children and they prophesy. The Lord's blessing is upon them. They will spring up among the grass like poplars by streams of water. One will say, "I am the Lord's," and another one will call on the name of Jacob, and another will write on his hand, "Belonging to the Lord."

I confess that my children are seekers of wisdom and understanding. They hold fast to Your Word and to Your ways. They treasure Your commandments, and they cry for discernment. The spirit of wisdom is poured out upon my children and my children's children, and words of wisdom are being made known to them.

The Lord keeps my family from falling and presents them blameless before the presence of the Father's glory with exceeding joy.

SCRIPTURAL REFERENCES: Joshua 24:15; Acts 2:17; 16:31; Ephesians 1:3; Deuteronomy 28:1-12; Psalm 5:12; 84:11; 91:1,10; 112:2; 127:3-4; 128:3; 144:12; Song of Solomon 2:4; Isaiah 8:18; 59:21; 44:3-5; 54:13-14,17; Matthew 5:6,8; 6:13; Proverbs 1:23; 2:2-3; Jude 24.